HANS K. STUDER · DAVID DUNSFORD

WORLD REVIEW

1970
the year in pictures

WORLD REPORTING LTD.

26 BLOOMSBURY WAY, LONDON, W.C.1

EDITOR-IN-CHIEF
Hans K. Studer, Zürich

INTERNATIONAL EDITORS
Nils Lodin, Stockholm
Kerttu Saarela, Helsinki

LAYOUT
Flemming Ljørring, Copenhagen

TECHNICAL CO-ORDINATION
Werner Häner, Zürich
Fritz Walser, Zürich

COLLABORATORS
Prof. Pierre Dhombres, Paris
David Dunsford, London
Gisli Olafsson, Reykjavik
Albert J. Scherpenhuyzen, Neuenhof
Erika Tavernini, Zürich
Bernard Volker, Paris

The front and back inside illustrations show the Swiss exhibit "Brilliant Structure" at the World Exhibition at Osaka (photo UPI) and Japan's holy mountain, Fuji (photo Erhard Hürsch).

ISBN 0 900826 01 0

Federal Germany's Foreign
Minister: *Walter Scheel*.

Chile's new President:
Salvador Allende.

Egypt's new President:
Anwar Sadat.

Israel's Prime Minister:
Golda Meir.

Cambodia's new Prime
Minister: *Lon Nol*.

Nigeria's President:
Yakubu Gowon.

Britain's new Prime
Minister: *Edward Heath*.

The Year in Retrospect

Although 1970 was without a sensational event matching the technological triumph of 1969, namely a landmark in history because men set foot upon the moon for the first time, nevertheless there was plenty of drama and excitement. After a decade devoted to the conquest of space, however, it was symptomatic that the inhabitants of the earth once more concentrated upon their own planet and realized with dismay that they were gradually destroying it. The safeguarding of the environment was proclaimed the most important task of the seventies.

The political events of 1970 were dominated by an unprecedented escalation of terror tactics. A dangerously spreading cult of political violence was the sign of a world-wide social crisis. 1970 demonstrated the impotence of those in power when faced by terror wielded by fanatical groups and splinter groups which did not flinch from attacking and killing innocent people. News of hijackings, kidnapped diplomats and the cowardly murder of hostages filled the newspapers day after day. The brutal deaths of Germany's Ambassador von Spreti in Guatemala, Labour Minister Laporte in Canada and ex-President Aramburu in Argentina were symptoms of a development with which the blackmailed governments and peoples were unable to cope. The world was forced to look on helplessly while the passengers and crew of three giant jets, hijacked into the Jordanian desert by Palestine guerrillas, were held for weeks under the threat of death. Britain's new Prime Minister Heath, in a speech to the 25th anniversary meeting of the U.N. General Assembly, made the gloomy forecast that the main danger of the seventies would be civil wars rather than wars between nations.

The dynamic attitudes of Federal Germany's first Social Democratic Chancellor Brandt and his liberal Foreign Minister Scheel made 1970 a forward-looking year for their country. For the first time in 25 years the Heads of Government of the two German states tried to bridge the gap between their countries, but the second inter-German summit meeting failed to fulfil the high results expected. A few days after Brandt had demonstrated Germany's willingness to atone for her past, by falling on his knees in front of the monument commemorating the rising in the Warsaw ghetto, Poland was shaken by a serious crisis which swept the country's leaders out of office.

Although 1970 saw the end of the Biafran conflict, it witnessed the extension of the war in Vietnam into Cambodia. After the guns had at last fallen silent along the Suez Canal, Arabs fought Arabs in the Jordanian civil war. Egypt, at a critical moment, poised between peace and war, lost her leader Gamal Abdel Nasser. And France mourned General Charles de Gaulle, Europe's last grand old man.

1970 also was a year of natural disasters. Hundreds of thousands lost their lives in the century's worst catastrophe, the devastating floods in East Pakistan. Fifty thousand were killed in a terrible earthquake in Peru. Cholera struck in Asia and Africa and penetrated as far as Europe. Floods in Rumania and a series of avalanches in the Alps caused much human suffering.

The death sentences after the political trials at Burgos and Leningrad caused a storm of indignation all over the world. This violent reaction persuaded the men in power in Madrid and in Moscow to exercise clemency. This victory for protest actions meant that, despite everything, 1970 ended on a note of conciliation.

January

Biafra is dead: As the population of Nigeria's Federal capital Lagos
celebrated the military victory over the breakaway province in the East,
Ibo soldiers, whose hopes have been crushed, queued for food after their
capitulation.

Biafra belongs to history. All the untold sufferings of the brave Ibo people, sacrificing two million dead to the dream of a state of their own, had proved in vain. Nigeria's strategy of starvation and the use of modern weapons against a badly equipped army were, in the last analysis, more potent than the national will which had sustained the "people's war" of the Ibos. The Biafran tragedy is a dark chapter in the history of Africa and of the human race. Great Britain supplied Nigeria with guns, armour and advisers because she was afraid the spark of successful secession by the eastern province might set alight other African states. The Soviet Union, hoping for a further bridgehead on the African continent, supplied General Gowon's military government with MIG jet fighters and Ilyushin bombers, piloted by Egyptians and white mercenaries among whose targets were hospitals and markets. Biafra obtained her arms supplies, albeit in much more modest quantities, from France and Portugal. The United States, for once, opted out of her self-appointed role of policeman of the world, although oil rights were involved, while the United Nations watched the bloody spectacle for two and a half years without taking action because, according to them, it was an internal Nigerian problem. Only when the whole thing was over did U.N. Secretary U Thant pay a visit to Lagos. There he changed his plan to fly to former Biafra in order to form his own view about the distress of the Ibos: more important matters made it necessary for him to proceed to Paris . . . .

Hardly had the curtain come down on the Biafran drama, following the wholly unheroic departure of General Ojukwu, when a new grim and bloody spectacle demanded the attention of the horrified international public. The scene this time was dominated by the gallows and the firing squad. In Baghdad, Baathist President Al Bakr handed over to the executioner 36 alleged conspirators whom he had lured into a trap by means of a trumped-up attempt at carrying out a coup.

January 1 Edward Kennedy inquest starts at Edgartown.
U.S. trade union leader Joseph Yablonski assassinated.
10 44-year-old Soviet cosmonaut Pavel Belyaev dies after operation.
12 Capitulation of Biafran Army after President Ojukwu had fled the country.
16 British Socialist M.P. William Owen arrested for suspected espionage.
Ghana expels one million aliens.
17 U.S. Vice-President Agnew returns from Asian trip to Washington.
19 First Indian nuclear power station is inaugurated.
20 Dutch Bishops declare in favour of relaxation of compulsory celibacy.
Talks between the United States and China resumed in Warsaw.
21 Thirty-six alleged conspirators executed in Iraq after pretended coup.
France declares her intention to supply Libya with 100 Mirage fighters.
22 Israeli troops temporarily occupy Egyptian island of Shadwan in Gulf of Suez.
Chancellor Brandt suggests negotiations to Prime Minister Stoph of the German Democratic Republic.
25 Alexander Dubcek arrives in Turkey as Czechoslovak Ambassador.
28 Oldrich Cernik replaced by Lubomir Strougal as Prime Minister of Czechoslovakia.

5th January: The last act of the drama of Chappaquiddick began at Edgartown in the State of Massachusetts, U.S.A. A legal investigation was started to clarify the hazy circumstances of the sensational accident which cost 28-year-old Mary Jo Kopechne, a Kennedy election helper, her life after a party. In front of the court building hundreds of reporters waited for Senator *Edward Kennedy*, her companion on the fatal drive. The principal witness took two hours to give his sworn testimony during the inquest held behind locked doors. After the judge had refused the application for exhumation of the girl's corpse, the grand jury decided to drop the case, despite unresolved contradictions.

5th January: The assassination of 59-year-old *Joseph Yablonski*, a trade-union official who, together with his wife and daughter, had been found riddled with bullets in his house in Clarksville, Pennsylvania, threw a gloomy light on conditions in certain American trade unions. With the triple murder the embittered power struggle for the control of the U.S. Mine Workers' Union assumed gangster-like dimensions. "Jack" Yablonski, member of the union leadership since 1942, wanted to dislodge Tony Boyle, its President, in order to cleanse the union of corruption and power politics. In December 1969 he stood as a candidate against Boyle—and lost "in one of the most dishonest elections in the history of the labour movement". The police were convinced that Yablonski had been killed by hired assassins.

This picture, one of the most sensational photographs ever taken in the Himalayas, was recorded by the Austrian expedition whose aim was the conquest of the 25,000 ft high Dhaulagiri IV, one of the last unclimbed peaks of the Himalayas. During the assault, however, Richard Hoyer, the leader of the expedition, four of his fellow Austrian mountaineers, and a Nepalese Sherpa were killed in a fatal accident. The breathtaking picture is taken from Hoyer's last remaining film: he photographed his friends *Peter Lavicke* (top of the picture) and *Kurt Ring* (below) on a frighteningly narrow ridge, with a 6,000 ft of abyss on either side. The mountaineers had agreed that, should one of them lose his foothold on the loose snow path, only a few inches wide, his companion on the rope had to throw himself down the other side to brake the fall of his partner.

7th January: The discussion about compulsory celibacy for
Roman Catholic priests reached a new climax during the Dutch
Pastoral Council at Noordwijkerhout. Despite the Pope's
eleventh-hour intervention, this national Catholic ecclesiastical
conference rejected the age-old tradition of celibacy for the first
time and voted by an overwhelming majority in favour of
allowing priests to marry. The Pastoral Council further agreed
to a proposal for the admission of women to the priesthood. The
Bishops, who participated in the discussion but not the voting (the
picture shows Cardinal *Bernardus Alfrink,* the Primate of the
Church in the Netherlands, during the discussion on celibacy)
proclaimed a few days later that in their view priests should enjoy
complete freedom of choice between celibacy and marriage—an
affront against Rome which, through the voice of Paul VI, had
implored the Council to eschew discussion of celibacy. The
Vatican was afraid the Dutch breach might cause the dam to
collapse.

12th January: After some delay —and several breakdowns— Europe, too, entered a new epoch of civil aviation: Pan American World Airways started operating, on scheduled flights across the Atlantic, the Boeing 747, the world's largest passenger aircraft. The revolutionary "Jumbo Jet", which few European airports were equipped to accommodate (the top picture shows the gigantic jetplane next to its smaller brother, the Boeing 707, at Orly airport, Paris) needs parking space as large as a football pitch. The colossus, showered with superlatives, is 230 ft long and 64 ft high; it has a wing span of 195 ft, and a maximum take-off weight of 322 tons. It is capable of carrying 362–490 passengers, depending on the seating arrangements (the lower picture shows the economy class). Suspended from the wings are the largest and most powerful engines ever built for an aircraft and the fuel capacity is 39,000 gallons. Twenty-eight airlines from all over the world have so far placed orders for 180 of these planes from the Boeing Company: the Jumbo Jets herald the start of another period of hectic competition in air transport.

12 January: The long-awaited collapse of the Biafran State came with surprising suddenness after 950 days of independence and the loss of countless lives. Employing new tactics and weapons the Nigerian Federal troops, carried out co-ordinated attacks on several fronts and subjected the shrinking jungle base to ceaseless bombardment with their Russian guns and bombers, finally breaking the resistance of the Ibos.
Declaring he was leaving "in search of peace" and would soon return, Head of State Ojukwu abandoned his people, forced to their knees by starvation, and Chief of Staff Effiong, the acting Head of State, offered Biafra's capitulation to the Federal government in Lagos. President General Gowon accepted and asked all Nigerians to welcome the former rebels as brothers. The end of the fighting meant that the bloody war of secession was over, but not the drama of the starving Ibo population (the picture below shows a British Red Cross worker with a child dying from starvation). There were only isolated excesses by the Federal troops flushed with victory, but since Gowon refused to authorize the continued air relief by the particularly effective Joint Church Aid and only reluctantly accepted the help of the Red Cross, the problems of food shortage remained acute.

During the final Nigerian offensive, leading to the occupation of Owerri, Ojukwu's last provisional capital, hundreds of thousands of Ibos fled into the bush but returned after Biafra's capitulation.

In his victorious mood Nigerian President Major-General *Yakubu Gowon* rejected foreign aid for the starving Ibos ("They can keep their blood-stained money—we don't want it and don't need it!"), but magnanimously promised not to treat the defeated rebels as second-class citizens, or to put their leaders on trial.

Before Biafran Head of State Ojukwu left Biafra for an unknown destination, he appointed Chief of the General Staff *Philip Effiong* as his representative. The 45-year-old Major-General, a member of the Biafran minority tribe of the Efik, had no choice but to capitulate: "The suffering of our people must be brought to an immediate end. The people are disillusioned." He asked Gowon for an armistice and declared: "Biafra no longer exists".

After three hours of negotiations Nigerian President, General *Gowon* and acting Biafran Head of State, General *Effiong* signed the document of capitulation in Lagos on 15th January. Gowon welcomed his former brother-in-arms with the words: "Glad to see you again, Philip!". The two generals laughingly slapped each other on the back after the formalities of the capitulation ceremony. This signified the official return of Biafra to the Nigerian Federation, which she had left on 30th May 1967 after Ojukwu's proclamation of independence.

Biafra's capitulation was preceded by the destruction and capture of the temporary airstrip at Uli by the Federal troops. This strip in the jungle (above) was Biafra's last link with the rest of the world. Aircraft with the markings of Joint Church Aid and of the International Committee of the Red Cross had made 7,342 landings on it, flying in altogether 81,300 tons of food and drugs in extremely hazardous conditions, mainly at night. The greatest humanitarian aerial supply operation of all times had been kept going at the cost of 16 ancient propeller-driven aircraft and 27 crew killed.

The man who once promised his people: "I shall never surrender, I shall never run away, and even if I am the last Biafran, I shall face the enemy with my rifle at the ready," abandoned his people in their most desperate hour. With his family, three tons of luggage and a white Mercedes, General *Odumegwo Ojukwu* fled from his jungle base aboard a Super-Constellation aircraft, leaving behind his emaciated soldiers, demoralized and leaderless (bottom picture, opposite). But even from his unknown exile Ojukwu appealed to the Ibos: "Since our cause is just, we believe that we have not lost the war. Only the battlefield has changed. As long as I am alive, Biafra lives." But Biafra was dead.

15

18th January: After his trip to East Africa which included State Visits to Kenya, Uganda and Tanzania, Archbishop *Makarios*, the President of Cyprus, went to Rome where, accompanied by his Foreign Minister *Spyros Kyprianou*, he called upon the exiled King *Constantine* of Greece. Since Makarios Had previously been to Athens and had discussions with Prime Minister Papadopoulos, it was assumed that he was attempting to mediate between the junta and the King, in favour of Constantine's return to the throne. Or he might have been trying to interest the young King in his new policy aimed at preventing the partition of the island state of Cyprus, recently afflicted by a new wave of terror, and to win over the island's Turkish population to accept reunion. He is seen here with Queen *Annemarie*, Crown Prince *Paul* and Princess *Alexia*.

22nd January: The Israel raid on the Egyptian
island of Shadwan was another move in the
psychological warefare between the two countries.
Israeli parachutists occupied the 10-mile long and
2-mile wide fortified island in the Gulf of Suez,
taking prisoners, destroying military installations,
and sinking two torpedo-boats of Soviet origin.
Dayan's commandos withdrew from the island
32 hours later. An Israeli military spokesman
declared that the attack on Shadwan had to be seen
as part of the military operations following Egypt's
decision not to observe the armistice. One month
previously a group of Israeli commandos had
dismantled a whole radar station of Soviet
manufacture at Ras Ghareb on the West coast of
the Gulf of Suez and taken it by air to Israel.

After a break lasting more than two years, the talks between the United States and China, started in 1954 in Geneva and transferred to Warsaw in 1958, were resumed in the Polish capital at ambassadorial level. U.S. Ambassador *Walter Stoessel*, leaving the Chinese embassy after the 135th meeting, told waiting journalists (bottom picture) that a number of subjects of mutual interest had been discussed, but that it had been agreed to treat the talks as private. The atmosphere of the talks had been factual. The next round of the dialogue took place at the U.S. embassy, but the Chinese Chargé d'Affaires *Lei Yang* (top picture, shown leaving the U.S. embassy), after the 136th meeting, was no more ready to talk than Stoessel had been. Before the resumption of the talks, the United States had made a number of gestures to "thaw" the relations with the People's Republic of China, including the relaxation of the 19-year-old trade embargo. Peking, in response, had displayed greater interest in establishing contacts with the world outside. The Warsaw talks were started at a time when the Soviet-Chinese negotiations in Peking had reached a bottleneck. But it still appears to be a long and stony path to a noticeable improvement or even normalisation of the relations between the United States and the People's Republic of China. In Peking's view, the biggest stumbling block was the American support of the Chinese Nationalist government of Formosa.

22nd January: Born in 1912 in Rumania and domiciled in Paris for several decades, the playwright, *Eugène Ionesco*, initiator of the "theatre of the absurd" and constantly surprising promoter of a theatrical anti-theatre, was elected to the Académie Francaise in recognition of his original contribution to contemporary drama. This meant that one of today's most performed authors (The Bald Primadonna, The Rhinoceros, The King Dies, Hunger and Thirst, The Chairs, Victims of Duty, etc.) entered the sacrosanct French Académie. In accordance with tradition, the new "Immortal" was received in audience at the Elysée Palace by the President of the Republic.

25th January: The disgraced former Czechoslovak Party Leader, *Alexander Dubcek*, whose political power had been gradually diminished, arrived in Turkey to take up his post as Ambassador of Czechoslovakia and a few days later presented his credentials to Turkey's President Cevdet Sunay. Despite his immense popularity, he had been branded a traitor of Communism, removed from the Party leadership and forced to give up the chairmanship of the Federal Assembly. An attempt by his most determined opponents to prevent the newly appointed ambassador leaving Prague had failed by a narrow margin. For his successors, Dubcek's diplomatic posting to the most easterly NATO country represented a compromise solution; for Dubcek himself it amounted to exile. The hero of the "Prague spring", who resolutely refused to deny his former actions, thereby forfeiting his seat on the Central Committee and bringing about his expulsion from the Party, knew only too well that the last word against him had not yet been spoken in Prague or Moscow.

23th January: The conservative wing of the Communist Party, faithful to Moscow, was once more firmly in charge of Czechoslovakia. In the course of a new purge directed against the last bastions of the progressives, Prime Minister Oldrich Cernik, also had to give up his post and resign from the Party Praesidium. Cernik, one of the exponents of the reform movement and, consequently also placed under arrest after the Soviet invasion of August 1968, had subsequently allowed himself to be converted to "realism" in an attempt to retain his political position and had even justified the invasion with the allegation that the country had been threatened by a counter-revolution. But even this cynical opportunism could not save him. His successor as head of the government was 45-year-old orthodox Communist *Lubomir Strougal* (above), who had been trained in the Soviet security services and was a former Minister of the Interior during the Novotny rule. As Deputy Party Leader he had long been preparing for the assumption of power.

28th January: The White House police, who had transformed themselves into a "palace guard" on the orders of President Nixon, paraded for the first time in their white tunics with gold trim during the reception of Britain's Prime Minister, Harold Wilson, in Washington. The Americans were extremely annoyed that the White House guards should have been dressed up in costly gala uniforms like musketeers in a musical comedy, which while enriching any performance of the "Merry Widow", were hardly appropriate for the seat of power in the United States, or in accordance with President Nixon's appeal to reduce expenditure.

February

An old friendship reaffirmed despite violent demonstrations: French President *Georges Pompidou* makes state visit to the U.S.A. to see President *Richard Nixon*.

World-wide indignation is shown over the callous attacks on civil aircraft: Dr. *Georges Habash*, Leader of the "Popular Front for the Liberation of Palestine" which acknowledges responsibility.

An extreme left-wing group of Palestinian terrorists boasted of the crash of a Swissair Coronado flying from Zurich to Tel Aviv as a victory in the struggle against Israel. After a world-wide wave of horror and indignation at this cowardly act of terrorism the "Unified Command of Arab Guerilla Organizations" denied the attack, whereupon the "General Command of the Popular Front for the Liberation of Palestine" also suddenly disclaimed responsibility. It seemed as if the more responsible leaders of the Fedayeen had become conscious of the boomerang effect of this kind of "warfare". The denial, however, appeared all the more unconvincing because of the fact that an aircraft of Austrian Airlines only just managed to escape the same fate as the Swissair Coronado on the same day: after an explosion detonated by the same method, the Caravelle succeeded in carrying out an emergency landing. In the latter case it was possible to trace back the outrage to Arab initiative beyond the slightest doubt. Likewise, the results of the careful and thorough scientific investigation of the catastrophe to the Swissair aircraft turned the suspicion of sabotage into near certainty. Was international air traffic to capitulate before these bomb-throwing desperadoes? After the outrage a categorical demand was raised for internationally respected agreements to ensure safety in the air. IFALPA, the International Federation of Air Line Pilots Associations, in view of the continued lack of action against the criminal activities of aerial pirates and terrorists, threatened a world-wide strike of their members. IATA, the International Air Transport Association, concerned about competition, failed to take any effective measures and ICAO, the International Civil Aviation Organisation, appeared the last hope. However, its machinery was slow getting into gear, and meanwhile there was the possibility of some "liberation movement" in the world terrorizing air traffic in order to gain their ends.

February 1 Railway catastrophe in the Argentine: 159 killed.

2 Bertrand Russell, the British philosopher, dies aged 97.

3 José Figueres elected President of Costa Rica.

10 Avalanche in Val d'Isère kills 39.

11 Japan becomes the fourth country to launch a satellite with own rocket into earth orbit.

12 Israeli bombing raid on Egyptian metal works at Abu Zabel kills 70.

13 Arson at Jewish old people's home in Munich causes seven deaths.

18 Chancellor Brandt states his readiness to meet the Prime Minister Stoph of the German Democratic Republic without preconditions.

21 Sabotage causes crash of Swissair Coronado, killing all 47 aboard. Austrian Airlines Caravelle carries out emergency landing after explosion.
Strategic "Plain of Jars" in Laos again in Communist hands.

22 Agreement between Hussein and guerilla leaders: Jordanian King to sack his Minister of the Interior.

23 Guyana becomes a republic but remains in the Commonwealth.

24 French President Pompidou on state visit in the United States.

27 Guatemala's Minister of Foreign Affairs Alberto Fuentes Mohr kidnapped by extreme left-wing rebels, released 30 hours later after guerilla leader had been set free.

28 Wedding of Nepal's Crown Prince Birendra in Katmandu.

An oriental atmosphere surrounded the spring collections of some Paris fashion houses. Louis Féraud, who presented his colourful new designs in a newly opened Paris Métro station, was particularly influenced by the "Harem fashion". Although the maxi had finally arrived, it was hardly to be expected that the emancipated woman of 1970 would hide her physical charms to the extent proposed by Monsieur Féraud.

2nd February: 28 young Ethiopians, studying at
Scandinavian universities, occupied their country's
embassy in Stockholm in protest against the violent
suppression of student demonstrations in Addis
Ababa. They tore down the flag and an emblem
from the balcony of the building and replaced it
with the banner "Territory liberated by the
Ethiopian people". The students, opponents of
Emperor Haile Selassie's authoritarian régime, then
proceeded to argue about freedom and democracy
with the Embassy staff for four hours. The Swedish
police brought the occupation to an end after the
Foreign Ministry in Stockholm had approached the
Ethiopian Government to ask for instructions.
The Ambassador himself had not asked for police
intervention.

2nd February: Bertrand Russell, the British
philosopher and mathematician, died at his home in
Penrhyndeudraeth, North Wales, at the age of 97.
This single-minded fighter for peace and humanity,
and descendant of an aristocratic family, had publicly
protested against conscription during the First
World War, and was sent to prison and dismissed
from his lectureship at Cambridge. In the thirties
he supported the Indian struggle for freedom. After
the Second World War the third Earl of Russell
largely devoted himself to the task of emphasizing
the dangers of the nuclear age: even at the age of
89 the convinced pacifist accepted a week's
imprisonment for instigating an unauthorized
sit-down by nuclear disarmers in Parliament Square.
The War Crimes Tribunal, which he founded, not
only condemned American crimes in Vietnam, but
also opposed the invasion of Czechoslovakia by the
Soviet Union. His last protest was directed against
the persecution of the Soviet writer Solzhenitsyn.
Bertrand Russell, co-author of "Principia
Mathematica", the standard work of modern logic,
was awarded the Nobel Prize for Literature for his
writings on philosophy.

The £2,400 income per head in the small Sheikdom of Abu Dhabi on the Persian Gulf is the highest in the world. Due to the extremely high profits earned from its oil resources, which were nearly £100,000,000 in 1969 and to enlightened government, this desert state of 40,000 sq. miles has made the leap from the Middle Ages to the 20th Century within a decade. Today it is a modern welfare state with a thriving economy, and a growth rate three times higher than Kuwait. Twelve years ago there were neither schools nor roads in Abu Dhabi, its 20,000 inhabitants, mostly fishermen, pearl divers and camel breeders, spent their energy in the age-old fight against sun, lack of water and drifting sand dunes. Since then the number of inhabitants has risen to 50,000 and the whole island, which is linked with the Arabian peninsula by a new bridge, has been turned into a gigantic construction site: modern blocks of flats, houses, schools, hospitals, health centres, office buildings, mosques,

The island of Das, the basis of operations for off-shore oil production, is symbolized by the gigantic torches of blazing natural gas, escaping with a roar from the pipes sticking out of the sea. So long as the black clouds of smoke continue to rise above the once uninhabited island, Abu Dhabi will continue to prosper. The capital was once a poor fishing village, with the palace of the Sheiks the only building having more than one storey (above right, one of its towers). Abu Dhabi's political future is less rosy than its economic one. The British Government's decision to withdraw from East of Suez by 1971, places this small State in a difficult situation and has forced it to build up a small army.

churches and a new airport are rising at an incredible pace (below centre). Poor families are given completely furnished houses on large estates free of charge. A new port and new factories are under construction as well as a large desalination plant to cater for the rapidly increasing demand for drinking water. A four-lane motorway 100 miles long crosses the desert to Burmaimi Oasis, which is also in the grip of this building fever. (The bottom picture shows the inhabitants of this oasis at a well.) The unprecedented progress has been made possible by the profits from oil production: after 10 years of prospecting and development work the oil companies in Abu Dhabi produced some 29 million tons of oil in 1969. Two-thirds came from the mainland and one-third from off-shore deposits where the oil is collected and loaded into tankers on the island of Das in the Persian Gulf.

3rd February: The Swedish welfare state suffered its first big strike since
1945. After the introduction of a new and complicated system of
piece-work rates, the miners of the three iron-ore mines of Kiruna,
Svappavaara and Malmberget started a wildcat strike joined by the dockers of
the Baltic iron-ore port of Lulea. The point at issue was not money, since the
5,000 strikers are among the highest paid miners in the world, but a crisis of
confidence between the Social Democratic workers and the Social Democratic
directors of the LKAB state iron-ore corporation which is the largest export
enterprise in Sweden with an annual turnover of £64,000,000.
The strike was a protest against the bureaucracy of the trade-union movement
and a revolt against the slide-rule mentality of the administration. The
miners' demand for a more human approach and treatment of their interests
found a great deal of sympathy among the Swedish people. Since the strikers
received a lot of financial support and the Social Democratic government
remained completely neutral, one of the most important public enterprises
was paralysed for more than two months, and affected the British and Belgian
steel industries. The two pictures show the spontaneous outbreak of the strike
which started with a sit-in and the moment when the trains carrying the ore
were once more rolling in the direction of Lulea and Narvik.

The bloody clashes between units of the Jordanian Army and the many Fedayeen operating against Israel from Jordanian territory were intensified. It signified a new test of strength between King *Hussein*, here being welcomed with demonstrative enthusiasm by his troops, and the guerrilla leaders who demanded a more bellicose attitude by the Government in Amman. The Hashemite King, despite the support of his army, had to abandon, after tough negotiations, his attempts to bring the activities of the partisans under his control and thereby spare his own country the fierce Israeli reprisals. Furthermore, he was obliged to sack his Minister of the Interior, General Mohammed Rassul Kilani, who had imposed restrictions upon the movements of the Fedayeen.

33

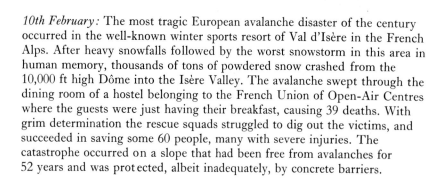

10th February: The most tragic European avalanche disaster of the century occurred in the well-known winter sports resort of Val d'Isère in the French Alps. After heavy snowfalls followed by the worst snowstorm in this area in human memory, thousands of tons of powdered snow crashed from the 10,000 ft high Dôme into the Isère Valley. The avalanche swept through the dining room of a hostel belonging to the French Union of Open-Air Centres where the guests were just having their breakfast, causing 39 deaths. With grim determination the rescue squads struggled to dig out the victims, and succeeded in saving some 60 people, many with severe injuries. The catastrophe occurred on a slope that had been free from avalanches for 52 years and was protected, albeit inadequately, by concrete barriers.

Two weeks after the catastrophe of Val d'Isère, a similar tragedy took place in the Swiss mountains. In the village of Reckingen, in Upper Valais, a gigantic avalanche, roared down from the Bächi valley in the early morning, sweeping away the officers' mess and five chalets of an Army camp. Although rescue operations started at once only 18 of those buried were rescued alive, some badly injured, leaving 19 officers and 11 villagers dead. The massive three-storey stone building in which the officers were quartered was completely destroyed and the débris swept 325 yds away. The last victim was not dug out of the snow until five days after the disaster. The rescue efforts—the top picture shows soldiers using sticks to probe for their officers in the snow—were hampered by the concrete-like hardness of the snow at the core of the avalanche. Snow continued to fall ceaselessly, severely hampering the rescue work and forcing the rescue teams to carry the victims through knee-deep snow to be laid out in the village (left). The last avalanche at this spot, which has a reputation for safety, occurred in 1743.

11th February: Prince *Charles*, heir to the British Crown, took his seat in the House of Lords for the first time. Wearing the traditional regalia, he was introduced into the House of Lords, sponsored by the Dukes of Kent and Beaufort, during a solemn ceremony lasting 15 minutes. Although the youngest person present, there was no one to compete with him as to his collection of titles, which include Prince of Wales, Duke of Cornwall, Duke of Rothsay, Earl of Chester, Earl of Carrick, Baron of Renfrew, Lord of the Isles and Great Steward of Scotland.

14th February: At 10 minutes past midnight the 47-year-old heart transplant surgeon, South African Professor *Christian Barnard* married 19-year-old *Barbara Zollner*, a millionaire's daughter of German origin. The ceremony was conducted by the Mayor of Johannesburg, in the house of the bride's parents in the Johannesburg district of Inanda. The heart surgeon had obtained a divorce from his first wife Louwtje in 1969 after 21 years of marriage. The only member of his family to attend the wedding was his daughter Deirdre, who is only two months younger than her step-mother. The same day the couple flew to Rome on their honeymoon.

Two criminal trials attracted an unusual amount of public attention. In the United States the harsh sentences in the Chicago conspiracy trial caused indignation throughout the country. The jury found five of the seven accused, guilty of the vague offence of "coming into the state with intention to incite violence", but acquitted them of actually having caused the disorders at the 1968 Democratic National Convention in Chicago. Nevertheless, 74-year-old Judge Julius Hoffman, who had shown himself incapable of maintaining the dignity of the court, condemned them to the maximum sentence of five years in prison, a $5000 fine and costs, with the proviso that they were to remain behind bars "to the last cent". The trial, which lasted four and a half months, degenerated into a judicial farce during which insults and obscenities were the order of the day. One of the accused found guilty was the yippie *Jerry Rubin* (right), who shocked the jury by giving the Hitler salute and celebrated his 31st birthday in the courtroom with birthday cake and burning candles. ("Yippies" originated from the gentle hippie movement and are activists working for a radical change in society.) The defence attorney of the "Chicago Seven", *William Kunstler* (above), was sentenced to four years in prison for contempt of court by Judge Hoffman.

Another international sensation was caused by the trial and sentence of 34-year-old *Erich von Däniken*, the Swiss author of the much-discussed best seller "Memories of the Future", translated into 16 languages, and of the hardly less successful "Back to the Stars". He was found guilty of having embezzled tourist taxes and raised loans with the help of forged documents. Although von Däniken had repaid the £39,000 he owed, out of his earnings, the court sentenced him to three and a half years in prison and a fine of £300 for repeated fraud, professional deception and forgery of documents. His best-seller, and the film based on it, attempt to give proof that our planet was once visited by travellers from outer space.

The Saigon government of General Thieu organized a "Tour de Vietnam" cycle race in order to prove to themselves, to the people of South Vietnam, and to the world at large that they really were in control of the country. Seventy-three cyclists, with a few exceptions all belonging to the Army, tackled the 800-km long race in stages from Nha Trang to Long Xuyen, in the Mekong delta. The Saigon government maintains that it controls 93 per cent of the population of South Vietnam, a statement which is open to considerable doubt. Despite this, they did not want to take any risks: the cyclists' convoy was closely guarded, troops along the route were alerted and three helicopters constantly circled above.

While a lull occurred in the Vietnam conflict and the negotiations in Paris got bogged down, the
"forgotten" war in Laos once more hit the headlines. Pathet Lao units and their North Vietnamese
allies, already in control of the whole of the North and East of the country, launched a large-scale
offensive and overran the Laotian government forces and the army of warlike Meo mountain
tribesmen, equipped by the CIA, in the strategically important "Plain of Jars". They occupied the
fiercely defended airfields of Xieng Khouang and Muong Suoi and came to a halt 13 miles from
the U.S. headquarters at Long Cheng. The U.S. Air Force carried out massive bombing raids in an
attempt to halt the Communist attack against the most important communications link in the country,
the road between the ancient royal city of Luang Prabang and Vientiane, the capital. The
Communist troops, however, using primitive means, constantly restored their supply lines (picture).
The Laotian régime of the once neutralist Prime Minister Souvanna Phouma, now supported by
Washington, had never appeared so close to collapse.

21st February: World-wide indignation was aroused by Arab terrorist attacks on civil aircraft, culminating with the crash of a Convair Coronado of Swissair, causing the death of all 47 passengers and crew aboard. An explosion and subsequent outbreak of fire occurred in the baggage compartment of the four-engined jet aircraft which had taken off for Tel Aviv from Zurich's Kloten Airport. Captain Berlinger and his crew made desperate efforts to save the plane and its occupants but, only a few minutes' flying time from Kloten, the returning Coronado crashed into a wood in the vicinity of the Swiss nuclear research reactor. The Captain's parting words from the smoke-filled cockpit of the stricken plane to flight control a few seconds earlier were: "There is nothing more we can do. Many thanks. Farewell." The site of the crash offered a view of total destruction (the bottom picture shows the head of the scientific service of Zurich's municipal police, Dr. *Max Frei-Sulzer*, an expert of international reputation, in front of the largest piece of structural wreckage to be found). A few hours after the crash the "General Command of the Popular Front for the Liberation of Palestine" claimed responsibility for the outrage. The unified command of ten Arab guerrilla organizations, formed only two weeks earlier, subsequently denied any Arab involvement in the catastrophe. In the course of the investigation during which even the most minute parts of the wrecked Coronado were re-assembled in a hangar at Kloten (top picture) the suspicion of sabotage turned into one of certainty. The most important piece of evidence was a badly damaged altimeter (found at the site of the crash) which did not belong to the equipment of the plane and which could have been used to detonate an explosive charge at a pre-determined height. The Swiss Federal Government reintroduced obligatory visas for the nationals of all Arab states and ordered stricter supervision at all airports. It also requested the International Civil Aviation Organization to convene a conference on security in order to call a halt to the senseless attacks on civil aircraft.

The denial by the Fedayeen was received with considerable scepticism, since a further attack was carried out on the same day against a Caravelle belonging to Austrian Airlines. Eleven minutes after take-off from Frankfurt Airport an explosive charge was set off in the cargo hold of a plane heading for Vienna, causing a gaping hole in the fuselage (above left). Fortunately Captain Thill succeeded in carrying out an emergency landing of the Caravelle, with its 38 occupants, at Frankfurt. The investigation clearly indicated that the explosive and the altimeter connected to it were hidden in a radio set which two Arabs had posted at Frankfurt as an airmail parcel to Israel. Apparently the attack had been planned against an El Al plane, but it was not realized that post for Israel was also carried by way of other airlines. Eleven days earlier the Federal Republic had already been the theatre of an "act of war" by Arab terrorists. Two Jordanians and an Egyptian, who had been ordered to seize an El Al plane carrying the son of Defence Minister Dayan, lobbed hand grenades into the transit lounge and an airport bus carrying Israeli passengers at Munich Airport, causing the death of one Israeli and injuries to nine others. The picture above shows the arrested Jordanian *Mohammed Hadidi* being led away for interrogation. His two accomplices, who sustained injuries during the attack, were also captured.

24th February: The state visit by French President *Georges Pompidou* to the United States was intended to mark a change of climate in Franco-U.S. relations since the departure of Charles de Gaulle. But even though during their first meeting at the White House (above) U.S. President *Richard Nixon* and his guest, reaffirmed the old friendship between the two countries and proclaimed their intention to strive after common aims, the visit was overshadowed by violent demonstrations in protest against the French government's Middle East policy. The boycott of Pompidou's address to Congress by Senators and Members of the House of Representatives and the wave of protests that followed him on his trip through the United States formed a strange contrast to the offers of friendship.

Claude Pompidou, France's elegant First Lady, saw her role during the state visit to the United States first and foremost as that of ambassadress of Paris haute couture. In her suitcase she carried 30 dresses representing the most recent creations of French fashion designers. For the gala banquet in the White House, Madame Pompidou wore a blue woollen coat with outsize cape over a richly embroidered organdie dress by Cardin.

Madame Pomp

WELL TRADE THE NEW YORK JETS FOR THE ISRAELI JETS ÉCHANGERONS LES JETS DE NEW YORK POUR LES JETS D'ISRAEL

Le président Pompidou

The demonstrations against French policy in the Middle East in general and the agreement to supply 100 Mirage fighters to Libya in particular assumed such massive dimensions that the French President considered a premature return to Paris (the picture shows President *Pompidou* and his wife, hemmed in by demonstrators, on their way to a reception at the Palmer House Hotel in Chicago. It was only the gesture of President Nixon, who decided at short notice to replace his Vice-President at a New York banquet in honour of the official visitor from France, which made him desist from doing so. As Nixon wittily remarked in his after-dinner speech, "this was the first time in American history that a President represented his Vice-President". He formally apologized for the incidents which had marred the visit of his guest.

28th February: The most sumptious wedding of the year took place on the "Roof of the World". In Katmandu, capital of the mountain kingdom of Nepal in the Himalayas, 24-year-old Crown Prince *Birendra* married 20-year-old almond-eyed Princess *Aishwarya.* She is a member of the once powerful Rana family which had ruled the country for a century, before being desposed by the grandfather of the Crown Prince in the fifties. Seven astrologers had calculated the most auspicious hour for the betrothal. The bridegroom, educated at Harvard and Oxford, headed the procession to the home of the bride on an elephant. The festivities, reminiscent of one of the tales of the "Arabian Nights", lasted three days.

March

First German summit conference at Erfurt between *Willy Brandt*, Federal German Chancellor, and *Willi Stoph*, Prime Minister of the German Democratic Republic: just another episode, or the decisive breakthrough in the East-West German question?

The German summit meeting at Erfurt was the first visible sign of the concerted policies of the new West German coalition government and its eastward-looking activities. The Secretary of State at the Chancellery, Egon Bahr, was negotiating with Soviet Foreign Minister Andrei Gromyko in Moscow on an agreement renouncing the use of force; the Secretary of State at the Foreign Ministry, Georg Ferdinand Duckwitz, was negotiating with Polish Deputy Foreign Minister Josef Winiewicz in Warsaw on the recognition of the Oder-Neisse frontier; and at Erfurt the inter-German dialogue was now resumed after 24 years. At the first meeting Willi Stoph demanded from Bonn that the official recognition of the GDR should form the basis of negotiations, while Willy Brandt was prepared, if need be, to pay this price in exchange for humanitarian concessions or a strengthening of the position of West Berlin. The contrasting points of view were already made clear by the composition of the two delegations: Brandt was accompanied by his Minister for All-German affairs to stress the inter-German character of the meeting. Stoph brought his Foreign Minister, thereby underlining the East German view that the contract was one between two sovereign states. Because of these fundamental contradictions there was very little elbow room for negotiations. Even the greatest optimists had to concede that it would take a long time to reach the stage of binding agreements.

Kidnapping, one of the underworld's most abominable crimes, was adopted as a weapon for use in political struggles by Latin American guerillas. The abduction of foreign diplomats signified the degeneration of internationally agreed procedures into jungle warfare. The murder of the kidnapped German Ambassador Count Karl von Spreti by extreme left-wing rebels in Guatemala recalled the worst atrocities of the middle ages and caused a crisis in the relations between Federal Germany and Guatemala. The Guatemalan government, which had been forced to ransom its own Foreign Minister in exchange for an arrested guerilla leader one month earlier, had not been prepared this time to release 25 political prisoners to save the life of the German diplomat.

Mr Ian Smith's proclamation of a Rhodesian Republic ended speculation on the future of the country. In reply the British Government demanded tougher sanctions, although it is doubtful if these would cripple the Rhodesian economy, and the Organisation for African Unity called on the United Nations to topple Mr Smith and his white regime by force.

March 1 Socialist victory in Austrian general election. Iceland becomes the eighth full member of EFTA.

2 Rhodesia proclaimed a Republic. Mr Clifford Dupont appointed acting President.

4 French submarine "Eurydice" lost with 57 men aboard.

5 Nuclear Non-Proliferation Treaty comes into force.

6 U.S. Commercial Attaché in Guatemala, Sean M. Holly, kidnapped by extreme left-wing rebels and released after three imprisoned guerilla leaders had been freed.

8 President of Cyprus, Archbishop Makarios, unharmed in attempted assassination in Nicosia.

11 Iraqi government reaches agreement with Kurdish leader Barzani.

12 Japanese Consul General in Sao Paulo, Nobuo Okuchi, kidnapped. Released in exchange for five political prisoners.

13 Cambodian ultimatum to Hanoi and Vietcong to withdraw their troops from Cambodia within three days.

14 Expo 70 opened in Osaka.

15 Former Cypriot Minister of the Interior, Polycarpos Georghadjis, assassinated.

16 Non-Socialist parties recover majority in Finnish General election.

18 Prince Norodom Sihanouk, Cambodian Head of State, deposed whilst on visit to Moscow.

19 First German summit meeting between Brandt and Stoph in Erfurt.

21 Colonel Carlos Araña Osorio elected President of Guatemala.

23 Coup in Congo-Brazaville fails.
Mr Arthur Chung sworn in as first President of Guyana.

24 U.S. Air Attaché in Santo Domingo, Colonel Donald Crowley, kidnapped. Released in exchange for 19 political prisoners.

25 Coup in Chile foiled.
Paraguayan Consul Waldemar Sanchez kidnapped in Argentina. Released despite government's refusal to free prisoners

26 Four-power talks about Berlin, the first after fourteen years.

27 The third Rumor government, a Left Centre coalition, announced in Italy.

28 Earthquake disaster in Turkey kills two thousand.

30 Failure of coup by Mahdi sect in Sudan.

31 Extreme left-Wing Japanese students hijack Boeing 727 of Japan Air Lines, forcing it to fly to Korea.
German Ambassador to Guatemala, Count von Spreti, kidnapped and murdered.
Soviet Marshal Semyon Timoshenko dies aged 75.

1st March: For the first time in the history of the Second Austrian Republic the Socialist Party emerged from a general election as the strongest party in Parliament, although it just failed to obtain an absolute majority. The Socialists won 81 seats whilst the People's Party, which had previously governed was reduced to 79 seats; 5 seats were won by the Freedom Party. 59-year-old SPÖ Chairman *Bruno Kreisky* (on the left, at his party headquarters on the evening of election day), became Chancellor designate and started negotiations with the People's Party about the formation of a grand coalition. These ended in an impasse, and Kreisky was sworn in as Chancellor of a minority cabinet, Austria's first purely Socialist government after a free election.

2nd March: One minute past midnight and 225
weeks after the unilateral declaration of independence
Ian Smith's Rhodesian Front proclaimed Rhodesia
a Republic. Prime Minister *Ian Smith* and
Rhodesia's first President *Clifford Dupont* (right)
signed the document introducing the new
constitution in Salisbury. This was the final phase
of the break with Britain who, assisted by the
United Nations, had made repeated attempts to
bring the rebellious colony to heel by economic
sanctions. After the Republic had been proclaimed,
the Smith regime consolidated its position by
holding a general election in which the Rhodesian
Front, representing the 225,000 white minority,
won all 50 seats reserved for whites. The five
million black population had to be satisfied with
16 seats.

At the same time as Rhodesia was severing her last links with the British Crown, another "Unilateral Declaration of Independence" was made to the British Government. The 11,000 inhabitants of the Isle of Dogs in the London borough of Tower Hamlets, an island in the Thames in the heart of London's dockland, declared its independence, after demands for better communications, more schools and improved housing had been ignored. *Ted Johns*, elected President of the "island republic" (shown in the picture, above left, flanked by his two Prime Ministers, *John Westfallen* and *Raymond Paget*) during a meeting of the government, explained the reason for their action: "We are better able to govern ourselves. The council of Tower Hamlets let the Isle of Dogs go to the dogs." Since no official notice was taken of the newly acquired independence the islanders soon got tired of their republic. Housewives collected signatures for a "Back to Britain" petition (above right) and soon the President and his two Prime Ministers returned to their ordinary jobs as office worker and dockers.

4th March: The French Navy suffered the loss of the submarine "Eurydice" with her crew of 57, which failed to return from an underwater trip off the southern coast of France. A geophysical institute recorded a violent explosion below the sea's surface and a search flotilla found oil patches and wreckage belonging to the lost submarine, which left no doubt as to the ship's fate. Seven weeks later the American research vessel "Mizar" located the sunken ship at a depth of 2,750 ft in the vicinity of Cape Camarat. Another boat, the "Minerve", in the same Daphne class (1,040 tons), had been lost with all hands in the Mediterranean in January, 1968. On that occasion President de Gaulle had joined the "Eurydice" in an underwater dive to honour the memory of the 52 crew who died in the "Minerve".

An unusual emergency landing was carried out by an air-taxi, with five people aboard, at the Swedish airfield of Norrtälje. During his approach to the runway the pilot discovered that one of the floats had fractured and was pointing downwards. The co-pilot Karl Andersen hung from the fuselage of the Cessna-185 (picture left) and by using his legs managed to keep the damaged float in a horizontal position thus avoiding a crash landing. The presence of mind and courageous action by the 44-year-old Danish co-pilot ensured a smooth touchdown.

After her separation from French film director Roger Vadim, film star *Jane Fonda* returned home to the U.S.A. and began to take an active role in politics. She declared her support for the "New Indians" who had escaped from their reservations and were preaching a doctrine of "Red Power". Basing their claim upon an ancient law, they had taken possession of the abandoned island prison of Alcatraz in San Francisco Bay. Their objective was to turn it into an Indian cultural centre for which they demanded government assistance. No longer content with being considered a colourful relic of the past the Indians wanted the white man to take them seriously and treat them as *de facto* partners.

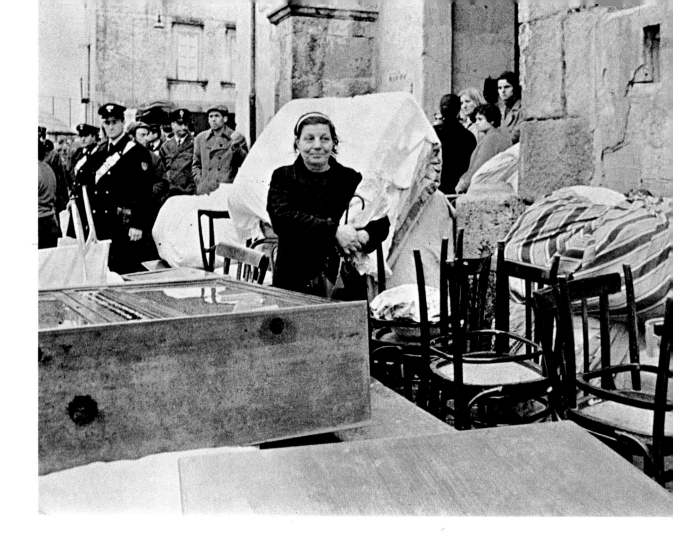

4th March: There was widespread panic in the port of Pozzuoli on the "dancing" coast of the Gulf of Naples after the authorities had asked six thousand inhabitants of the dilapidated Terra district, in the harbour area, to evacuate their homes which were threatened by an earthquake. A further 30,000 inhabitants, out of the total of 65,000, frightened by a succession of minor tremors, fled of their own accord. They were afraid they were sitting on a volcano which could erupt at any moment. The coast of Pozzuoli literally rose from the sea. Detailed measurements of this natural phenomenon indicated that the harbour area had risen by 37 inches during the previous eight months, and that simultaneously there had been a subsidence of the coast of the island of Ischia opposite. Many buildings sustained dangerous cracks and whole streets in the slum quarter were in danger of collapsing. Schools, shops and factories closed. The government prepared contingency plans to evacuate the remaining inhabitants by ship and train in the event of an emergency. However, since there were no spectacular developments in Pozzuoli for several weeks, tens of thousands of refugees returned home.

Incredible scenes took place in Pozzuoli at the height of the panic. Thousands stormed the town hall, where free rail tickets and payments of about £20 were handed out to the evacuees. Meanwhile others steadfastly refused to leave their houses and had to be evacuated by force. Many feared they might suffer the same fate as the Sicilian earthquake victims who, two years after the catastrophe, were still living in dilapidated huts while waiting for new houses and flats, which the government had promised to build for them.

The Temple of Serapis, dating from Pozzuoli's period of Greek influenced architecture, was one of the most precise indicators of the rising land levels. The pillars of the temple, a famous tourist attraction, rose from the sea by nearly 39 inches during the last few months.

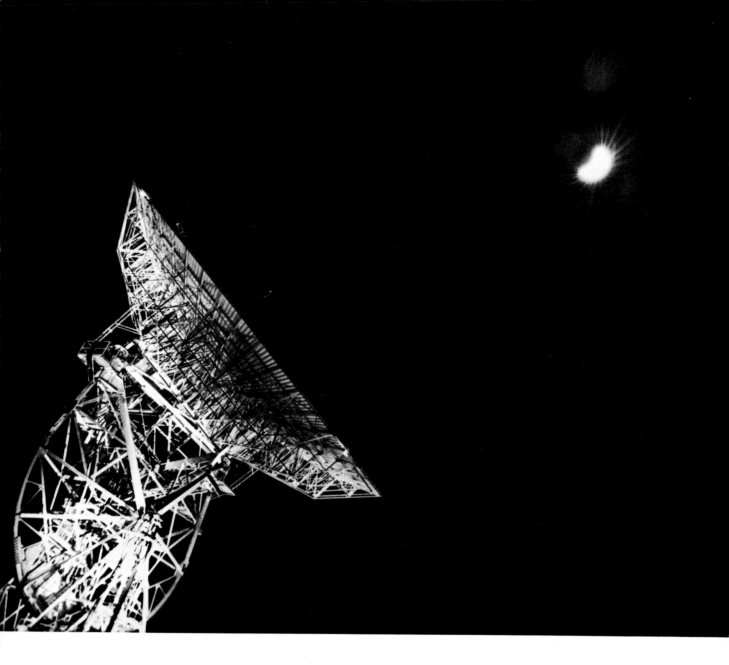

7th March: At 10.30 a.m. local time, Mexico experienced a total
eclipse of the sun lasting three-and-a-half minutes. Twenty minutes
earlier the moon had begun to move slowly in front of the sun,
darkening the sky, until the sun was completely obscured and
day turned to night. Within the area of the eclipse the stars
appeared in the blackened sky; a sudden drop in temperature was
registered; and in some cities people celebrated the event by dancing
in the streets.

8th March: The President of Cyprus, Archbishop *Makarios*, narrowly escaped an attempted assassination. Shortly after daybreak he took off in a helicopter from his residence in Nicosia to fly to the monastery of Makheras 30 miles away, where he was to celebrate Mass. But the helicopter had hardly risen from the ground when it came under machine-gun fire from the roof of a nearby school building. Pilot Zacharias Papadoyannis, a Greek Air Force officer and for three years the President's personal pilot, succeeded in landing the plane, riddled with bullets, behind the Presidential Palace despite being critically injured in the stomach. The attackers made good their escape with the aid of smoke-bombs. The police suspected members of the extreme right-wing underground "National Front" who, encouraged by the Junta in Athens, wanted union with Greece. Makarios (shown in the top picture examining the bullet marks in the helicopter) was considered the main obstacle to Enosis. After the attempted assassination Makarios's former Minister of the Interior and Minister of Defence *Polycarpos Georghadjis* (shown with his family in the lower picture) was placed under house arrest and banned from leaving Cyprus. The 40-year-old politician, once a leading figure in the EOKA resistance movement and subsequently considered the "strong man" of the government was lured a few days later, to an ambush by a telephone call and murdered. His body was found, riddled by six bullets, in his car on a secluded track outside the capital. There were all the signs of a vendetta. The identity of those responsible was less simple than in the attempted assassination of Makarios, since there were many groups who had an interest in the elimination of the devious and politically ambitious Georghadjis.

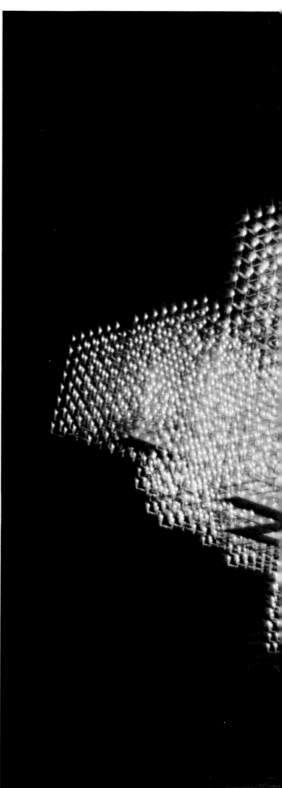

14th March: The first world exhibition in an Asian country was opened during a spell of icy cold weather. Expo 70, with the theme "Progress and Harmony for Mankind" was both a shop window for Japan and a world exhibition of superlatives. The site at Osaka covered a record area of 800 acres in the Senri hills within the boundary of Japan's second-largest city. After a construction period of one and a half years, the site was transformed into a gigantic showplace for 77 nations. A further 31 pavilions built by large Japanese industrial enterprises confronted the visitors with the world of today and to-morrow. The inauguration ceremony was graced by a gigantic robot moving about the central festival plaza. 50 million people are expected to visit Expo 70 from all over the world during the next 183 days.

On the left a panoramic view of Expo 70. The juxtaposition of
many different types of pop and exhibition architecture are fused
here into an impressive whole, dominated by the 360 ft high "Red
Cathedral" of the Soviet Union, typical of the craze for the colossal.
In the left foreground the Canadian Pavilion and the spherical
pavilion of the Federal Republic of Germany. Below left a nocturnal
view of two Japanese industrial pavilions: the seven storey copy of
the famous Todaiji Pagoda at Nara built by the computer industry
and the futuristic pavilion of the gas industry designed by the
Spanish artist Juan Miró. Among the most original creations at
Expo 70 was the "Brilliant Structure" of Switzerland (below). A stylised
tree of lights made of steel and aluminium 72 ft high and 180 ft
wide, it reflected the sunlight a thousandfold during the day and,
with its 32,036 lamps, glowed brightly at night.

16th March: The Finnish general election resulted in the parties of the Left losing their parliamentary majority, gained four years earlier. The number of Conservative seats increased by eleven to 37. However, the sensational victor of this election was 57-year-old *Veikko Vennamo*, Leader of the Smallholders' Party and up to that time their sole representative in parliament. He now returned at the head of a sizeable group of 17 deputies. Facing the press on election night, he was unable to disguise his elation at having achieved his revenge against the badly depleted Agrarians, who had expelled him from their party in 1958.

18th March: The political balancing act of Cambodia's Head of State Prince *Norodom Sihanouk* (right) came to a sudden end. For years he had astounded the world, irritated the great powers and safeguarded the rather tarnished neutrality of his small buffer state in the Indochinese cauldron. While the "People's King" was on a trip to Paris, Moscow and Peking, his Prime Minister, General Lon Nol, and Vice-Premier Sirik-Matak assumed power. Sihanouk, accused of having tolerated the infiltration of Communist troops, was deposed by the Crown Council and the National Assembly. The capital Phnom Penh, had previously been the scene of several violent demonstrations against the infringement of Cambodian sovereignty by Vietcong and North Vietnamese troops, during which the diplomatic missions of Hanoi and the Provisional Revolutionary Government of South Vietnam were stormed and ransacked (below). The new government rode on this wave of popular hostility against everything associated with Vietnam.

After Sihanouk had been deposed, President of the National Assembly *Cheng Heng* (below, on left) was sworn in as the new Head of State in accordance with the constitution. In his inaugural address he stated that Cambodia would continue her policy of independence, neutrality and territorial integrity and respect all international obligations entered into by his predecessor. Meanwhile in Peking, Sihanouk branded his successors as an extreme reactionary clique and "lackeys of American imperialism". He swore to fight the new régime "from within and without" until it was overthrown.

19th March: Willy Brandt, Chancellor of the Federal Republic of Germany, and *Willi Stoph*, Chancellor of the German Democratic Republic met to continue the inter-German discussions which had been abruptly ended 24 years ago. The handshake between the two German premiers at Erfurt station, before the start of their first meeting, was an historic event (below). The negotiations at the "Erfurter Hof" started with declarations of principle by both sides, which, as expected, revealed a large number of conflicting attitudes. While the representative of the German Democratic Republic made the demand for official recognition of East Germany his main point, the Federal Chancellor strove for the regularization of peaceful co-existence between the two German states within the 1970 boundaries and, above all, the alleviation of the human consequences of partition. Accompanied by East German Foreign Minister Otto Winzer, Brandt laid a wreath in memory of the victims of National Socialism in the former concentration camp of Buchenwald. Meanwhile Stoph met Walter Ulbricht, Chairman of the Council of State, in nearby Suhl, for a confidential two-hour talk aimed at finding a common denominator for further negotiations. The attention of the whole world was turned to this ancient city of Erfurt, in the "green heart of Germany", where Napoleon I and Goethe had once met. Would the first German summit meeting achieve the decisive breakthrough in the problems of the two Germanys ? The most important result of the meeting, was the decision to continue the dialogue at a later date. Stoph accepted Brandt's invitation to pay a return visit to Kassel on 21st May. It was, at any rate, more than an isolated episode. As the special train of the Bonn delegation returned to the frontier station of Bebra at midnight, the Federal Chancellor stated with satisfaction: "This day has enriched me."

The outbreak of spontaneous enthusiasm by the people of Erfurt was a moving human experience for Federal Chancellor Brandt. This clearly indicated to the world's press, assembled at Erfurt, why the GDR leadership had been dragging its feet over talks with Brandt. It was far more convincing than the hastily organised counter-demonstration cheering Willi Stoph and the people's army, and demanding that Brandit should give recognition to the GDR.

South Africa's participation in world sporting events suffered a further setback because of their Government's doctrine of apartheid.

After South Africa's refusal to grant a visa to the American tennis star *Arthur Ashe* (above left) to play in the South African tennis championship because he is coloured, the seven country committee (above) which organises the Davis Cup Tournament came to the inevitable decision to ban South Africa from taking part in the 1970 Davis Cup.

This move was initiated by the United States representative Robert Colwell who said that if South Africa took part it "would endanger the running of the competition".

Meanwhile in England controversy increased over the June visit of the South African Cricket Team. *Peter Hain* (right), Chairman of the "Stop the Seventy Tour", stepped up the campaign to hold demonstrations, whilst the M.C.C. President Maurice Allom and Secretary Billy Griffiths (below), repeatedly confirmed that the tour would go ahead. Cricket pitches where the matches were scheduled to be played were patrolled by police and dogs as well as being surrounded by barbed-wire, to prevent damage.

21st March: French lorry drivers successfully revolted against their government's ban on vehicles over $3\frac{1}{2}$ tons passing through towns. With hundreds of lorries the indignant drivers blocked the main roads in and out of Paris (the picture shows the Carrefour des Quartre Chemins in the suburb of Pantin) and important intersections throughout France, bringing traffic to a standstill. In the the resultant traffic jams even the police trying to clear the roads were themselves immobilized. The Chaban-Delmas government was forced to decree a drastic reduction of the ban it has imposed.

The 15th Eurovision Song Contest in Amsterdam was won by the 18-year-old singer and music student *Rosemary Brown*, called *Dana*, from Londonderry (left). The song, "All Kinds of Everything", was more like a folksong than modern pop music. It was the first victory for Ireland. Although the Scandinavian countries refused to take part in the contest, the programme was watched by more people than ever before: it was televised by 21 West and East European countries as well as Tunisia, Israel and, for the first time, via communications satellite, Brazil, Argentina and Chile.

24th March: While tension was rising once more in Ulster, where only the presence of British troops prevented renewed clashes between Catholics and Protestants, the young M.P., *Bernadette Devlin* (second from the right), together with other civil rights campaigners, protested outside No. 10 Downing Street in London. Their 14-hour vigil was against refusal of the government to investigate the circumstances of the death of a Catholic worker, Sam Devenney, father of nine children. Suffering from tuberculosis and a weak heart, he is alleged to have been beaten up in his house by several policemen, after street fighting in the Catholic Bogside quarter of Londonderry. He died three months later after several heart attacks. As a result of the protest the case of Sam Devenney was debated by both Stormont in Belfast and the House of Commons in London.

The Fiji Islands, which achieved their independence in October, were the scene of a Royal visit from London. On the way to what was to prove a triumphant tour of Tonga, Australia and New Zealand, Queen *Elizabeth II*, Prince *Philip* and Princess *Anne* visited the "Happy Isles" in the South Seas. They were given an enthusiastic welcome in Suva, the capital (top right). Even the rain did not dampen the joy of the Chieftains who waited patiently beneath their sunshades to be presented to the Royal Family (bottom right). Less restricted by court etiquette than her mother, Princess Anne, was a carefree ambassadress of the London mini-dress fashion which, although on the wane, had made a hit with the younger generation all over the world.

28th March: Turkey was again struck by a catastrophic earthquake. During the night a sudden and heavy tremor, resembling a "gigantic hammerblow", destroyed the town of Gediz in Kutahya province, and 500 villages in the area. The inhabitants, who are used to earthquakes, were taken completely by surprise. Buildings not affected by the first tremor were destroyed by fires, which spread rapidly despite continuous rain, and by a whole series of subsequent tremors. Large new multi-storey buildings, as as well as small houses of the older type collapsed. The catastrophe caused 2,000 deaths; another 3,000 people were rescued from the ruins alive but injured. In all 170,000 people lost their homes, possessions and economic means of survival. The old woman (picture right), who had lost the rest of her family during the night of terror, sat crying in front of the ruins of her home, in the stony desert of Gediz, with the few belongings she had managed to dig out. The feeding of the survivors, their housing in emergency accommodation and future reconstruction posed tremendous problems for the Turkish authorities. An international rescue action was launched immediately to help alleviate the heart-breaking suffering.

31st March: Japan's first hijacking incident was the longest and most dramatic in history. Nine members of the extreme left-wing "Red Army" student faction, with Samurai swords and explosives, took over a Boeing 727 belonging to Japan Air Lines, with 131 people aboard. The pilot who had left Tokyo bound for Fukuoka in Southern Japan was forced to set course for North Korea. Negotiations during an intermediate landing in Fukuoka led to the liberation of 23 of the women and children aboard. The top picture on the right-hand page shows them leaving the hijacked plane, supervised by a hijacker brandishing a Samurai sword. After five hours the hijackers forced 47-year-old Captain *Shinji Ishida* (above right, at the window of the cockpit), a much-decorated former pilot in the Imperial Air Force, to continue the flight to Pyongyang. Over the 38th parallel Ishida established contact with North Korean flight control but subsequently landed, to his own surprise, at Kimpo Airport, Seoul, capital of South Korea (above left). In the meantime the airport had been dressed up to look like North Korea. South Korean emblems had been replaced by painted signs reading "Welcome to North Korea", and North Korean flags. When the plane landed soldiers in North Korean uniform hastened towards it (bottom right) and girls in North Korean dress prepared to greet the hijackers with flowers. Unfortunately the extremely well staged deception miscarried because an official failed to stand his ground during an idealogical cross-examination by the hijackers. There followed a war of nerves, lasting several days, during which the abductors threatened to blow up the hijacked aircraft unless they received permission to take off for Pyongyang. In the end they agreed to release the 99 exhausted passengers and four air hostesses in exchange for Japan's Deputy Minister of Transport Yamamura, who had offered to join the plane as a hostage. On 3rd April the hijackers, with three members of the crew and the Minister, flew to Pyongyang. The kidnapped Japanese were found guilty of illegal entry after formal legal proceedings but, in view of the exceptional circumstances, received no punishment. After a number of contradictory statements North Korea agreed to release the jet plane and allow it to return to Tokyo. The extradition of the hijackers was refused.

After the return of the hijacked Boeing
727 to Tokyo's Haneda Airport the hero
of the hour was 36-year-old Deputy
Minister of Transport *Shinjiro
Yamamura*: He had volunteered, after
75 hours of negotiations between the
hijackers and Japanese government
officials at South Korea's Kimpo
Airport, to act as hostage aboard the
the plane. Representatives of the
government and the opposition and a
large crowd gave Yamamura and the
crew an enthusiastic welcome. The
picture left shows Yamamura (right
front) with Minister of Transport
Tomisaburo Hashimoto (with glasses),
Foreign Minister *Kichi Aichi* and Head
of Protocol *Shigery Hori*.

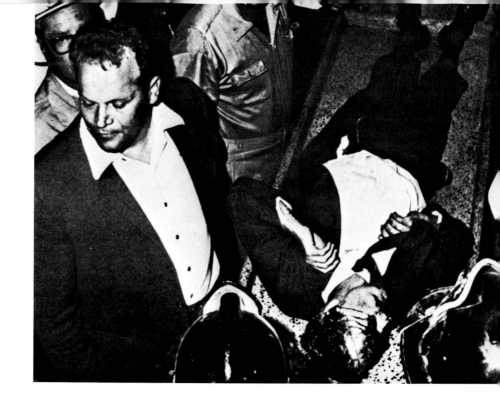

31st March: Kidnapping as an instrument of political blackmail found imitators in Latin America. During the month of March alone, revolutionary guerillas kidnapped five diplomats in Latin American capitals to enforce the liberation of political prisoners. The escalation of violence and counter-violence, terror and counter-terror, reached a new climax with the murder of Count *Karl von Spreti*, West German Ambassador to Guatemala. The 62-year-old diplomat had been dragged from his Mercedes in front of his house and abducted by six guerillas of the extreme left-wing "Rebel Armed Forces" (FAR) to an unknown destination. At first the kidnappers demanded the release of 16 prisoners as ransom, but later raised their price to 25 prisoners and £300,000. The hesitation of the Guatemalan government, pleading legal reasons, cost the Ambassador his life. Six days after his abduction he was found shot dead in a dilapidated hut outside the capital (the top picture shows an official of the German Embassy identifying the victim). The Papal Delegate, Mgr. *Gerolamo Prigione*, headed the procession to the National Palace where von Spreti's remains were to lie in state. Bonn's Foreign Minister, Walter Scheel, later escorted the body of his murdered subordinate back to Germany.

April

Dramatic life and death struggle in space: the service module of the Apollo 13 spacecraft, ripped open after the explosion of an oxygen tank.

The fight for the safe return of the astronauts has been won: Apollo 13 Commander, *James Lovell*, with his wife *Marilyn*.

After 22 successful space flights, there was less interest in the United States for the Apollo 13 mission. This situation, however, was suddenly transformed when the explosion in the service module of the spacecraft threatened to turn the astronauts Lovell, Haise and Swigert into the victims of a space disaster. The 85 hours of mortal danger made people realize that manned space travel remains a hazardous venture and that technology has its limits, even if, in the end, it saved the three astronauts. During those hours the computer was the best friend of the astronauts. Only electronic brains could cope with the complicated calculations for new flight routes, necessitated by the emergency return to earth, within the short period available. The rocket engine of the lunar module "Aquarius" which, 330,000 km from the earth had become a "lifeboat", ensured the safe return of the men from space. Once more it was shown that astronauts are not robots but courageous men and highly skilled technicians who, in a moment of mortal danger can decisively tackle and master dangerous situations.

The Americans suffered an unexpected blow to their space programme as a result of the Apollo 13 crisis. It was decided to postpone the next flight to the moon, originally planned for October 1970, until early in 1971. A few days after the American space drama, the People's Republic of China celebrated its space premiere. This event, with its extensive military and strategic implications, was bound to have an effect on the negotiations between the United States and the U.S.S.R. on the limitation of rocket armaments. Meanwhile Mao's artificial moon circled over Washington, London, Paris —and Moscow, chirping its Chinese revolutionary hymn "The East is Red" . . .

April 10 90 Vietnamese massacred in the Cambodian internment camp at Prasot.

11 Launching of the U.S. spacecraft Apollo 13 with astronauts James Lovell, Fred Haise and John Swigert.

13 Greek Government frees Mikis Theodorakis.

14 Explosion in the service module of Apollo 13: moon landing cancelled.

15 Soviet economy strongly critized by Brezhnev.

16 Second round of U.S.-Soviet SALT talks start in Vienna.
Sanatorium in Savoy buried by landslide: 71 killed.

17 Precision splashdown of command module "Odyssey" in the Pacific: successful conclusion of the Apollo 13 mission which had almost ended in disaster.
New massacre in Cambodia; 150 Vietnamese killed in Takeo internment camp.

18 Disorders in Bogota after the Colombian presidential election, narrowly won by Misael Pastrano Borrero.

20 President Nixon announces the withdrawal of another 150,000 U.S. troops from Vietnam by May 1971.

21 Swearing-in of Socialist minority cabinet in Vienna after failure of coalition talks.

22 Soviet Union celebrates 100th anniversary of Lenin's birth.
Cambodia appeals for help to the U.S.A. and the United Nations.
After grave disorders, state of emergency declared in Trinidad.
General election in South Africa: National Party again retains majority.

24 Launching of first Chinese satellite.
Unsuccessful coup by Haitian navy.

29 Israel accuses Soviet Union of direct participation in the Middle East conflict: Soviet pilots protect Egyptian airspace.

30 South Vietnamese and U.S. troops enter Cambodia.

7th April: It was with tears of emotion that *John Wayne*, the tough hero of Westerns for forty years, received his first Oscar at the prize-giving ceremony of the American Motion Picture Academy. The 62-year-old movie veteran was awarded the most coveted film trophy in the world for his portrayal of the drink-sodden marshal in "True Grit". Although Hollywood was in the throes of its worst economic crisis since becoming the hub of the film industry, it once again displayed the glitter of its heyday for the 42nd Oscar awards.

7th April: Svetlana Alliluyeva, the 44-year-old daughter of Joseph Stalin, who, having been deprived of her Soviet citizenship, became a millionairess after publishing her book "20 Letters to a Friend", married 57-year-old American architect *William Wesley Peters*. The wedding, only twenty days after their first meeting, was conducted in accordance with Quaker rites at Taliesin West, the architectural college in Arizona directed by Peters. The new son-in-law of the late Soviet dictator was previously married to a daughter of Frank Lloyd Wright, the great American architect. She lost her life in a car crash in 1946 and her name, too, had been Svetlana.

9th April: A sudden gale struck Genoa causing a dreadful maritime disaster. The 15,900-ton British ore freighter "London Valour" was dashed against a breakwater and badly holed in the bows. Ninety minutes later this modern turbine-driven ship sank in the turbulent sea, churned up by the "Libeccio", the dreaded south-westerly gale. The performance of the rescue crews was exemplary, the equipment at their disposal less so. Although firm land was only a few feet away, 20 of the ship's crew of 58 lost their lives in the inferno; only four of those rescued were uninjured.

In Cuba, bearded Prime Minister *Fidel Castro* (with sun glasses pushed up) demanded a 10 million ton sugar-cane crop. With the harvest in full swing he joined the "Macheteros" to encourage them. However despite the mobilization of all available forces, Castro had to admit four months later that, with a harvest of 8·35 million tons of raw sugar, the target had not been reached. The excessive effort to attain this target had caused a dangerous imbalance of the economy with possible far-reaching consequences. The hopes of economic prosperity during the next five years now look doubtful. "The leaders of the revolution have served an expensive apprenticeship," he declared in a three-hour speech on the 17th anniversary of the start of the Cuban revolution. "We deserve to be called ignorant. You can sack me, if you want to."

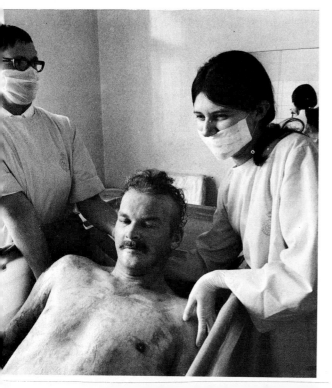

As recently as ten years ago a person who sustained burns to his skin of more than 40% was doomed to death. Since then the chance of survival has been raised beyond the 70% limit. Now, thanks to a new method of treatment, the Karolinska Hospital in Stockholm is able to report a sensational breakthrough. After an explosion in the harbour at Stockholm, *Riku Roupsa*, a workman, was taken to the hospital last November with 85% burns. A team headed by Dr. Sten-Otto Liljedahl engaged in the seemingly hopeless fight to save his life. The patient was placed on a specially designed heated bed and given 26 litres of liquid during the first 24 hours, subsequently 10 litres a day. In addition the patient was treated with antibiotics to prevent infection and carefully washed every day. He had to undergo a total of six operations, each time skin taken from dead people was transferred to his body. Five months later he was discharged with no disfiguring scars.

11th April: After four successful flights to the moon and two successful landings on the planet, the American public was already getting somewhat bored by the time the spacecraft Apollo 13 was launched. After hours of uncertainty, the U.S. space agency NASA, only 24 hours before the planned launching, decided to go ahead on schedule with the venture which had been in doubt for some time because of an outbreak of German measles. Thomas Mattingly, who was not immune against German measles, was replaced as pilot of the command module "Odyssey" by his stand-in, John L. Swigert (38), who joined the experienced James A. Lovell (42) and space novice Fred W. Haise (36) on their lunar mission. Many superstitious people had reservations about the flight on account of the number 13. A photographic reporter recorded as a gimmick, but not as a bad omen, the ominous frequency of this figure as the Saturn V rocket with the Apollo 13 spacecraft on top, took off 13 hours, 13 minutes, 13 seconds from the start of the countdown. As the gigantic projectile blasted off 0·6 seconds late from the launching pad at Cape Kennedy, the copy-book start, by now routine, succeeded in dispelling all secretly held fears.

In friendly fashion *Thomas Mattingly* (top picture, left), who was susceptible to German measles and had therefore been replaced 24 hours before the launching, gave his stand-in *John Swigert* final hints for the steering of the "Odyssey". Swigert, like Mattingly, was a bachelor and thus became the first unmarried astronaut in space.

The German Federal Chancellor, *Willy Brandt* (centre), was present at the Cape Kennedy launching with U.S. Vice-President *Spiro T. Agnew* (left). Professor *Wernher von Braun*, creator of the moon rocket Saturn V and now NASA Director of Planning, was also present, standing behind the German Chancellor.

330,000 km and three days' travel away from the
earth an explosion in the service module of
Apollo 13 created the most dangerous situation in
the history of American space travel. "We have a
problem here," reported the astronauts after a
warning light indicated that something was
radically wrong. They discovered that the contents
of one of the three oxygen tanks was emptying into
space and causing the spacecraft to roll, a
movement which was controlled only with difficulty.
In addition the fuel cell gauges were also recording
zero. The astronauts, whose training for emergencies
had prepared them for all conceivable crises,
reacted with lightning speed. They carried out the
required manoeuvres and climbed into the lunar
module "Aquarius" which took on the role of a
lifeboat in space. Three hours after the explosion
all supplies of current and oxygen, and thus also of
cooling and drinking water, from the damaged
service module to the now largely crippled command
module broke down completely and the astronauts
were in mortal danger. It was not until the service
module was jettisoned, shortly before re-entering the
earth's atmosphere, that the full extent of the
damage was revealed. The photograph above taken
by the astronauts showed a 4-metre long hole in
the service module.

In a flash the indifferent attitude of the American nation to space travel was changed when the alert was signalled. With bated breath the whole world followed the space drama, the most nerve-racking and costliest rescue action in history: an estimated $50 million a day. The planned landing on the Fra Mauro plateau of the moon had to be abandoned immediately after the explosion, although Apollo 13 was forced to follow a return orbit round the moon since, at the time of the explosion, the spacecraft was only some 77,000 km away from the planet. For 85 hours the astronauts were in extreme danger and people all over the world wavered between hope and fear until the rescue operation ended successfully with a precision splashdown in the southern Pacific, within sight of the recovery vessel "Iwo Jima". The recovery of the astronauts—Swigert is shown here being hoisted from the rubber dinghy to the helicopter—only took 45 minutes. The three men, despite their exertions, were in surprisingly good condition.

Together with naval chaplain Commander *Philipp Jerauld*, aboard the aircraft carrier "Iwo Jima", *James Lovell, Fred Haise* and *John Swigert* (from the left), said a prayer of thanksgiving. Afterwards Lovell admitted "There were moments when we thought we might never return".

In Hawaii, President *Richard Nixon* honoured the astronauts by awarding them the highest civilian honour of the United States, the Medal of Freedom. The first to receive the medal was *James Lovell*, who has spent a total of 715 hours in space, longer than any other human being.

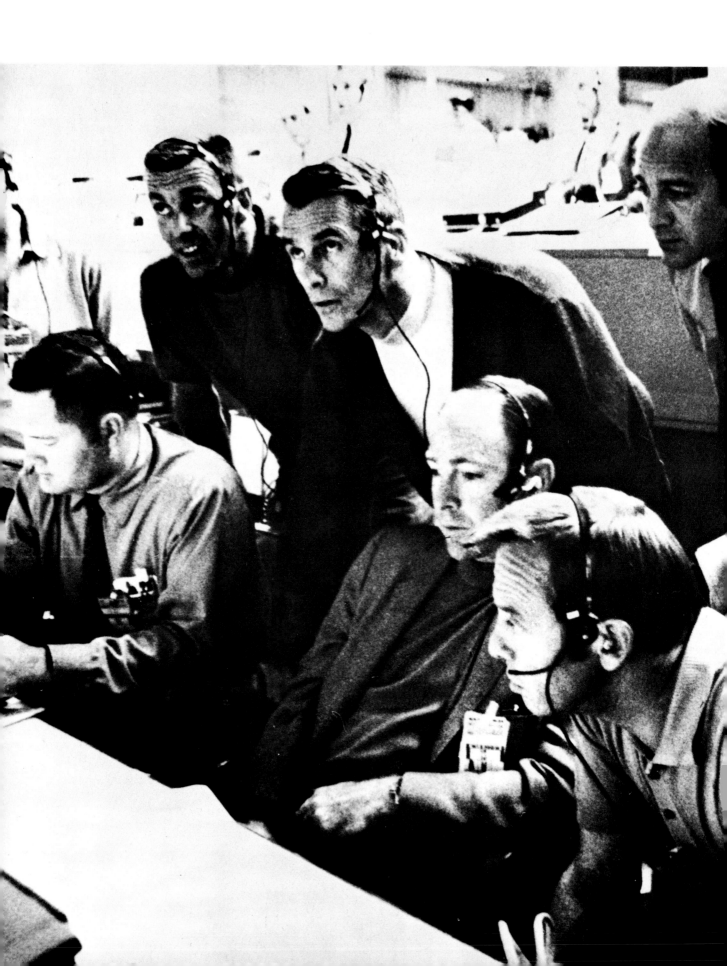

The Apollo 13 astronauts owed their safe return to earth not only to their admirable composure and courage, ruling out the possibility of panic in the spacecraft, but at least as much to the part played by the concentrated application of both human and electronic brains on the ground. Supported by a battery of computers, a whole army of experts at Houston calculated all imaginable alternatives for the unplanned return to earth. Each movement of the stricken spacecraft and every reaction of its crew was monitored by instruments. The picture left shows, standing, the astronauts *Anthony England, Joe Engle, Eugene Cernan* and *Ronald Evans;* seated, from the left, Flight Director *Raymond Teague* and Apollo 14 astronauts *Edgar Mitchell* and *Alan B. Shepard*. After splashdown the oppressive tension dissolved into tears of joy. At Houston spacecraft centre President *Nixon*, accompanied by his wife *Pat* (above left), presented the happy wives of the Apollo 13 astronauts, *Marilyn Lovell* and *Mary Haise* (in the seventh month of her pregnancy), to the cheering crowd. Subsequent investigations lasting several months disclosed that the cause of the fatal breakdown in space had been the failure of two minute thermostat switches which had been wrongly connected up during a test countdown.

13th April: Thanks to the intervention of the French journalist and politician Jean-Jacques Servan-Schreiber the Greek Government, in a surprise move, released the famous composer *Mikis Theodorakis*, who had been imprisoned since 1967, and permitted him to leave the country. The 44-year-old composer of the film music for "Zorba the Greek" and "Z" was allowed to fly to Paris to receive treatment for his tuberculosis. This popular musician, who had been a member of parliament for the communist EDA Party and the leader of the left-wing Lambrakis youth movement, had for a long time been a thorn in the side of the Colonels' régime as a symbol of intellectual resistance against the military dictatorship. A few days after his arrival in Paris Theodorakis held a press conference (above) and appealed for resistance to the Papadopoulos government. He also took part in the Labour Day procession in Paris (right). Subsequently his wife, *Myrto*, with their two children, *Jorgo* and *Margarita* (the picture shows them in their home in Athens) succeeded in escaping to Italy in a small boat.

The Greek junta having tried to boost their image abroad by the release of Theodorakis, continued their dictatorial measures to maintain law and order. Trials of opponents to the régime followed in quick succession. Great interest was aroused, both inside Greece and abroad, by the trial of 34 intellectuals before a special military court in Athens. They were accused of being members of the underground "Democratic Defence" movement and of having planned the overthrow of the régime and having carried out bomb outrages. Some of the accused, supported by fearless defence advocates, accused the judicial authorities of brutally torturing them whilst awaiting trial in prison. The principal defendant 40-year-old *Dionysios Karagiorgas* (left), formerly a teacher of political science, for whom the public prosecutor had demanded the death penalty, was sentenced to life imprisonment. He had lost a hand when a home-made bomb exploded in his flat. It was this accident that caused the police investigations of this group of academics, lawyers, engineers, judges, students and senior officers. The other two defendants in the picture, *Emanuel Deloukas* (centre) and *Christos Rokofilos*, were each sentenced to 13 years' imprisonment.

16th April: After the avalanche disasters earlier in the year at Val d'Isère and Reckingen, the western area of the Alps was struck by the third and most dreadful mountain catastrophe of this winter of terror. At the mountain resort of Plateau d'Assy in Savoy, a landslide engulfed two wards and two staff buildings of the tuberculosis sanatorium "Le Roc des Fiz" soon after midnight. The solid concrete structures were struck by the "black avalanche", and crushed like match boxes, being swept 50m down the slope and buried under rocks, tree-trunks, snow and earth. 71 people were killed including 56 boys. The black avalanche had started from the Rochers des Fiz (2,300m) and swept aside a forest of fir trees, intended as a barrier. The rescue teams were confronted by a hopeless scene as they began their work at dawn.

18th April: The presidential elections in Colombia resulted in grave disorders after the Government had proclaimed their Conservative candidate *Misael Pastrano Borrero* the winner. He is shown here during an election trip in the north-eastern part of the Latin American Republic being presented with an attractive headgear by an Indian princess of the Goajira tribe. When the narrowly defeated former dictator Gustavo Rojas Pinilla was placed under house arrest, his supporters revolted and tried to storm the Presidential Palace in Bogota. The Government had to declare a state of emergency. A recount confirmed Pastrano Borrero's victory by 56,000 votes.

22nd April: Anniversary celebrations for the birth of *Vladimir Ilyich Ulyanov*, the man who transformed a whole world. The Soviet Union celebrated, with tremendous festivities, the 100th anniversary of the birth of Ulyanov, better known by his adopted name of *Lenin*, leader of the October Revolution and creator of the U.S.S.R. His gigantic portrait dominated Red Square in Moscow where the mausoleum of the idol of the Communist movement is located. Even on this day, however, the ideological armistice continued between the U.S.S.R. and China. While Brezhnev, the Soviet Party Leader, during a festive session in the Kremlin, accused the "nationalist policy of the Chinese leadership" for the split in world Communism, Peking deplored "the treason committed against Leninism by the Soviet revisionist renegades" and called for the overthrow of the Soviet leadership.

One of the most tragic fates ever suffered by a people was that of the Armenians who achieved their own independent state for only a short period after the First World War. The bloody persecution and suppression of their national movement by the Turks, which culminated in frightful massacres in 1895/96 and 1914/15 must be counted among the saddest episodes in the history of mankind during the last hundred years. 20,000 Armenians gathered on the Bikfaya hills near Beirut, in the Lebanon, in order to unveil a monument which is to serve as a reminder of these darkest hours in the life of their people.

24th April: Pope *Paul VI* visited the
Mediterranean island of Sardinia,
one of the most poverty-stricken areas
of Italy. 200,000 faithful congregated
in Cagliary in order to catch a glimpse
of the Head of the Roman Catholic
Church. In his address the Pope
described the fate of the population
of Sardinia as deplorable, and
exhorted the Bishops on the island
to ensure that, in times of radical
social change, the people should not
lose their faith. In the slum quarter
of Sant'Elia there occurred the first
violence during a papal visit. Young
anarchists, engaged in a hunger strike
against the construction of luxurious
tourist accommodation, threw stones
at the column of papal cars, hitting
the vehicle of Cardinal Villot and
some police cars on escort duty.
As a result fourteen people were
injured and twenty-two arrested.

24th April: To the surprise of the whole world, the People's Republic of China entered the space-age by launching its first earth satellite. Weighing 173 kg, twice as heavy as the first Russian sputnik and twelve times as heavy as the American Explorer I, its elliptical orbit round the earth took 114 minutes. The nearest the satellite "China I" came to the earth was 439 km, the farthest away was 2,345 km, and during its orbit it broadcast the revolutionary hymn "Tung fang hung" (The East is Red). China is the fifth country after the Soviet Union, the United States, France and Japan, to launch an earth satellite into space. The experts differed as to whether "China I" had been launched into its earth orbit by an intercontinental rocket or a modified medium-distance rocket. Pictures of the space launching were not made available for publication by Peking, except those showing cheering, delighted crowds (the picture here shows secondary schoolchildren listening to a radio report of the launching of the "Mao Moon").

Christies, the London auctioneers, held the biggest jewel auction in the world in the ballroom of the Hotel "Richmond" in Geneva. During the two hours of the sale, 386 pieces changed hands for a record price of £1,335,000. The climax of the gathering was the auction of two magnificent diamond earrings belonging to an "ex-queen" (there was talk of ex-Queen Soraya) which fetched the record sum of £205,000.

May

The last remaining oasis of peace in Indo-China is sucked
into the vortex: the devastated and looted city of Tonle Bet.

President Nixon, in order to shorten the Vietnam conflict, temporarily extended it into an Indo-China war. That, at least, was how he explained to the American nation his reasons for carrying the war into Cambodia. The fact was that Nixon could not stand idly by as the North Vietnamese and Vietcong, challenged by General Lon Nol, the new "strong man" in Phnom Penh, turned the whole of Cambodia into a base for attacking South Vietnam. This would have upset his time-table for withdrawal of troops and interfered with the Vietnamisation of the Vietnam war. The South Vietnamese, however, who entered Cambodia with the Americans, were less interested in the Vietnamization of the Vietnam war than the Vietnamization of Cambodia. The military régime in Saigon, full of self-confidence, did not hide its appetite for annexation.

In the United States the invasion of Cambodia triggered off a violent storm of indignation, the most serious to confront the otherwise prudent Nixon administration.

The opponents of the war, constantly growing in number and influence, accused the President of driving South-East Asia further and further into a political and military cul-de-sac and, by his arbitrary action, causing a further escalation of the war. Nixon was conscious that his intervention in Cambodia had placed his whole political career at risk. He declared that he stood by his order, even if this meant that he might not be elected to serve a second term. He added that he rejected all political considerations, because he did not want to be known in the history of the United States as the President during whose term of office America had become a second-rate power and accepted the first defeat in its proud 190-year history. The death of four students at Kent University shot by police, victims of the embittered atmosphere in the United States, certainly had not entered into the President's calculations. But had he considered the 50,000 Americans who had given their lives in Indo-China, since 1961, for a cause sustained by fewer and fewer people in the United States?

May 4 Four students shot dead on the campus of Kent University, Ohio, by men of the National Guard, during demonstrations against America's intervention in Cambodia.

5 Exiled Prince Sihanouk forms Cambodian Government in Peking.

6 New treaty of friendship and assistance between Soviet Union and Czechoslovakia signed.

12 Israeli military operation lasting 32 hours against the Lebanon in retaliation for guerrilla attacks.
The International Olympic Committee nominates Montreal (summer) and Denver (winter) as the venues for the 1976 Olympic Games and expels South Africa from its ranks.

14 Negotiations for the formation of a new Finnish government fail; President Kekkonen appoints Teuvo Aura, Mayor of Helsinki, to head a caretaker cabinet.

16 Joaquin Balaguer re-elected President of the Dominican Republic.
The Indonesian General Subardjo executed as leader of the 1965 rebellion.

17 The Cambodia conference in Jakarta demands withdrawal of all foreign troops and an end to hostilities in Cambodia.
Flood disaster in Rumania.

19 U.N. Security Council condemns Israel for attacking Southern Lebanon.

21 Second German conference between Brandt and Stoph in Kassel.

24 Reconciliation in Yemen after eight years of civil war.

25 Switzerland arranges for exchange of diplomats between Peking and Phnom Penh.

27 NATO Council works out a "strategy of relaxation". Proposal to Warsaw Pact countries for exploratory discussions on troop withdrawals in a limited area of Central Europe.

28 Victory of left-wing coalition in Ceylon General Election. Mrs. Bandaranaike Prime Minister for the second time.

29 Franco Maria Malfatti, Italy's Minister of Posts and Communications, elected successor to Jean Rey of Belgium as President of Common Market Commission in Brussels.
Argentina's ex-President General Pedro Aramburu kidnapped by Peronists.

31 Earthquake disaster in Peru kills 50,000.

1st May: Ten days after President Nixon had forecast the withdrawal of a further 150,000 U.S. troops from Vietnam, he ordered U.S. fighting units, accompanied by South Vietnamese troops, to attack the Communist-held areas along the border of nominally neutral Cambodia thereby widening the Vietnam conflict into an Indo-China war. (The picture shows U.S. armoured forces searching for North Vietnamese and Vietcong units during the westward advance through the Fish Hook area.) Nixon's unilateral decision to extend the war in South-East Asia in order to shorten it caused a political world crisis and deepened, more than ever before, the political controversy in America which had been only partly stilled by the slow but steady withdrawal of the GIs from Vietnam.

From the beginning of the Vietnam conflict the Cambodian Head of State, Prince Sihanouk, had performed a balancing act between Washington and Hanoi. Despite constant reference to the strict neutrality of his militarily weak country, he had permitted the North Vietnamese and Vietcong troops to establish bases and supply lines in the eastern border area. In return the Communists had left him alone. The *coup d'état* of 18th March put paid to the bold balancing act: General Lon Nol, Cambodia's new strong man, demanded the immediate withdrawal of the Communist troops from his country. This request, which the Communists treated as a declaration of war, had precisely the opposite effect. The Communists advanced against the capital, Phnom Penh, and subjected the Cambodian Army, consisting of 35,000 inexperienced troops, to strong pressure. The Cambodians took revenge by turning on the defenceless Vietnamese minority who were accused of collaboration with the Vietcong and interned in camps. The age-old rivalry between Cambodians and Vietnamese came to a head in a campaign of hate which culminated in bloody massacres. Hundreds of Vietnamese corpses floated down the Mekong river (below). For the first time North and South Vietnamese were in agreement. While Hanoi increased its military pressure upon Phnom Penh, the Saigon Government protested against the bloody persecution of its compatriots. The Lon Nol régime, in increasingly serious trouble and having gradually lost as much as a fifth of Cambodia's territory to the Communists, appealed to the United States and the United Nations for assistance against the foreign aggressors.

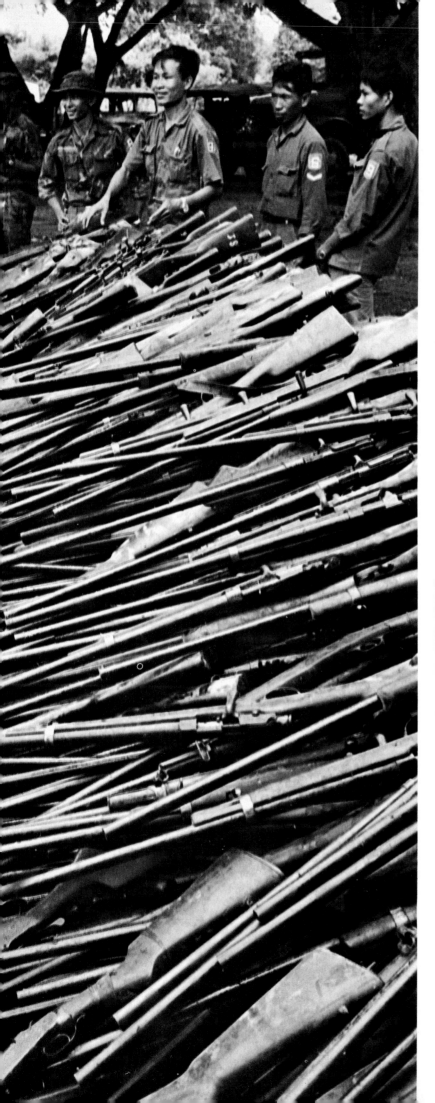

President *Nixon* told the American people on radio and television about his decision to march into Cambodia (below). The reason he gave for the controversial step was the concern of his generals that the Communist successes in Cambodia seriously endangered the U.S. troops in Vietnam. He publicly stated that he would stand by his decision even if this meant that he might not be re-elected to serve a second term as President. However, Nixon undertook to withdraw all his troops by the end of June and set territorial limits for the action. Although the Americans and South Vietnamese failed to find the headquarters of the Communists, they unearthed and destroyed extensive underground hideouts and stores of food and arms. The picture left shows arms captured after the occupation of the provincial capital Kompong Speu.

Moscow and Peking reacted strongly against the American intervention in Cambodia and accused Washington of violating the 1954 Geneva agreement on Indo-China. During his first press conference since he took office, Soviet Prime Minister *Alexei Kosygin*, in the presence of his Foreign Minister, *Andrei Gromyko* (top picture), declared that nobody had given the United States the right to behave as the world's policeman. He ended all speculations about the reconvening of the Indo-China Conference by stating that it was time to act, not to talk. The Indonesian Government, in an effort to mediate, tried to convene a conference on Cambodia in Jakarta. Since it was boycotted by the Communist countries, it remained powerless and was unable to achieve anything beyond recommending the withdrawal of all foreign troops from Cambodia. Despite this exhortation, the hostilities continued. The 43,000 South Vietnamese soldiers behaved like occupiers in a foreign country rather than allies. The picture above shows the battle for Kompong Cham; on the right American armoured troops are seen guarding Vietcong prisoners captured during the fight for Prasot. Opposite: The Khmer kingdom, hitherto so peaceful, has now become familiar with all the horrors of war. The people who had persecuted the Vietnamese minority during the events leading to the Cambodian campaign were now subjected to the harsh fate of refugees.

Nixon's decision to intervene in Cambodia abruptly ended
the tacit "armistice" between government and opponents
of the war on the U.S. home front. The indignation at
the extension of the war was strongest in the universities,
causing violent demonstrations. The most serious
incidents occurred at Kent University in Ohio. In the
course of demonstrations lasting several days the building
of the Army Cadet School was burnt down, whereupon
a state of emergency was proclaimed and the National
Guard called in. When the students, despite the
prohibition issued by the University President, once more
gathered on the campus, the men of the National Guard
attempted to disperse the crowds with tear gas (above).
This had no effect and the stone-throwing students
became more and more aggressive. The troops withdrew
to a hill, assumed offensive positions and opened fire
without warning. Four students, including two girls,
were killed; several others received serious injuries (right).

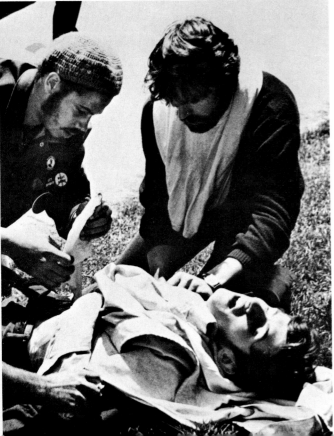

The shooting on the campus of Kent University deeply shocked the American nation. Nixon's Special Representative for Youth Questions, Anthony Moffett, demonstratively resigned in protest against the "vicious tactics" of the government. While Walter Hickel, the Secretary of the Interior, in a letter released for publication, warned the President about the growing alienation between young people and the government.

America was affected by a very serious moral crisis. The confidence gap, which had already separated the White House from a large section of the population during the Johnson administration and had prevented the consensus hoped for by the President, was now wider than ever. New York's Mayor Lindsay uttered the gloomy warning: "The country is practically on the point of spiritual and possibly even of physical breakdown." Other well-known politicians, including Senators of both parties, did not take this dramatic view, but considered Nixon's arbitrary action, by which he had by-passed Congress and caused a constitutional crisis, a tragic error. A mere handful of hawks approved of the invasion as a "necessary step". The crisis in the relations between the President and the American intellectuals reached its climax when Nixon referred to the students opposed to his Indo-China policy as "bums". During a massive anti-war demonstration in front of the White House (above) they retorted by comparing Nixon with Adolf Hitler. At this critical juncture the President swerved from his collision course and acted in a more conciliatory fashion, although he was determined to carry out his policy. It was at this moment that after mounting criticism from all sides he received support from an unexpected quarter. In a noisy patriotic demonstration, 150,000 New York building workers, dockers, civil servants and white-collar workers proclaimed: "We support our President, our country and our soldiers in Vietnam" in approval of Nixon's Indo-China policy (right). This demonstration also showed hostility to the rebellious students and Mayor Lindsay. At last the "silent majority", whose support Nixon and Vice-President Agnew had so readily appealed to made itself heard . . .

To show his conciliatory attitude, President *Richard Nixon* went as far as he could. He even engaged in an improvised discussion with a handful of students who, in anticipation of the large anti-war demonstration in Washington, had gathered in front of the Lincoln Memorial and were surprised to have an informal conversation with the President of the United States (left). Nixon had been unable to sleep and, at 5 o'clock, made the spontaneous decision to drive into town and talk to the students. During this encounter he tried to convince his sceptical listeners that he was attempting to achieve precisely what they wanted: an early withdrawal of all U.S. fighting men from Vietnam and a quick termination of the war with a minimum of losses. "I shall do what I can to initiate a dialogue with youth," Nixon said to a journalist, "but there is so much noise that it is difficult to make oneself heard."

16th May: After a bloody election campaign with an average of one political assassination per day the incumbent *Joaquin Balaguer* won a remarkable victory in the presidential election in the Dominican Republic. He received more votes than all his four opponents put together. Beneath Goya's famous "Nude Maja" the re-elected President (right) received the journalists at his residence in Santo Domingo; next to him is *Carlos Goico,* the new Vice-President.

5th May: For the first time since the intervention of the Warsaw Pact states in August 1968, when troops marched into the country, the Soviet Prime Minister *Alexei Kosygin* visited Prague. On his visit, made on the occasion of the celebrations commemorating the 25th anniversary of the liberation of Czechoslovakia at the end of the Second World War, he signed a new treaty of friendship and assistance (the picture of the signing shows, from the left: Prime Minister *Alexei Kosygin,* General Secretary of the Communist Party *Leonid Brezhnev,* CSSR Party Leader *Gustav Husak,* and Prime Minister *Lubomir Strougal;* standing behind, in the centre, President *Ludvik Svoboda*). The new treaty spelled out the forced adaptation of new home and foreign policies to meet the Kremlin's wishes. Brezhnev, the creator of the doctrine, received the order of "Hero of Czechoslovakia" from the aged President Svoboda and heard himself praised once more by Husak for the invasion and the "generous aid against the threatening counter-revolution . . ."

21st May: The second meeting between Chancellor *Willy Brandt* and *Willi Stoph*, the Prime Minister of the German Democratic Republic, took place at Kassel (the picture shows the two heads of government after the arrival of the East German delegation, behind Stoph, on the left, Bonn's Minister for Inter-German Relations, *Egon Franke*). Both within and without the conference chamber in the Schlosshotel Wilhelmshöhe, the course of the second German confrontation was far from smooth. It proceeded against a background of left-wing and right-wing demonstrations, which conveyed a wholly distorted picture of political life in the Federal Republic. Embarrassing incidents interfered with the planned programme. The very different attitudes of the two sides already foreshadowed by the first declarations of the two heads of government, deepened despite two *tête-à-têtes*. Brandt's attempts to ease the flow of discussion by submitting twenty points for negotiation, in reply to Ulbricht's draft treaty, failed because of Stoph's intransigeant "all or nothing". Stoph held to his maximum demand of "full diplomatic recognition before anything else" without giving the slightest hint of what kind of second step would follow this first one. Brandt, on the other hand, would not yield without being granted humanitarian concessions and the removal of traffic barriers. The meeting was adjourned for an indefinite period: no date was agreed upon for a renewal of discussions. Reporting to the Bundestag, Brandt declared there would have to be a pause for reflection to overcome the stagnation in the inter-German dialogue.

The conference had hardly begun when three young people, members of the "Deutsche Jugend des Ostens", armed with forged press documents, succeeded in reaching the flagpole of the Schlosshotel, where they hauled down the East German flag and tore it up. Stoph indignantly protested against the desecration of his country's flag.

The Communists, who had travelled to Kassel from all over the Federal Republic, were far superior in numbers to the right-wing extremists. They noisily demanded immediate recognition of the German Democratic Republic. At the memorial to the victims of fascism, supporters of the Communist Party and of the National Democratic Party came to blows. The laying of a wreath by Stoph had to be postponed for several hours when the police lost control of the situation.

Willi Stoph took his leave from *Willy Brandt* with the unexpected farewell "Auf Wiedersehen", although no further meeting for the two Prime Ministers had been arranged. Next to Stoph in the picture is his Foreign Minister *Otto Winzer*, who had just returned from Algeria, the 23rd country to grant East Germany international recognition. He confidently stated: "We shall see the day when Bonn, too, will grant our request for international recognition."

The sudden thaw in the snow-covered Carpathian mountains caused the already swollen rivers in Rumania to burst their banks, resulting in the worst floods in memory. 176 people were killed, while 276,340 people in 1,500 different localities lost their homes and had to be evacuated (below, left, shows flooded Satu Mare). Some 40,000 houses were wholly or partialy destroyed, together with 250 industrial premises. 900,000 hectares of agricultural land were flooded and 28,000 head of cattle drowned. The material damage was immense and the economic development of the country was set back several years. *Nicolae Ceausescu*, President and Party Leader, spent days touring the disaster area (below, right, in Braila, which suffered particularly), promising the population aid for reconstruction and tax concessions. Foreign countries also gave assistance, particularly the People's Republic of China which has maintained friendly relations with Rumania for many years. Proud of its independence the country was safe from a visitation by Soviet troops on manoeuvres for some considerable time because of the floods. But there was mounting concern that Moscow might employ economic pressure to force the afflicted country to fall into line with Soviet policies. Hungary also suffered from the floods. The picture opposite shows a farmer in the Csenger area rescuing his cattle.

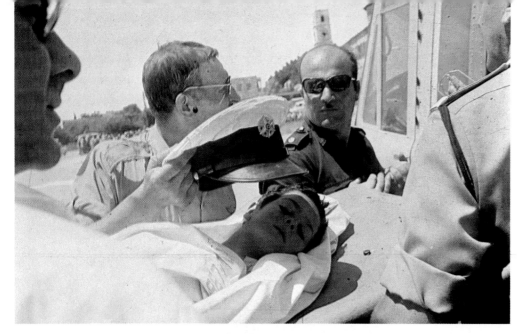

22nd May: In the Middle East the blood-stained drama of terror, revenge and counter-terror continued inexorably. Apparently in revenge for the bombing in error by Israeli Phantom Jets of an Egyptian village school in April, reported to have caused the death of thirty children, Arab guerrillas attacked an Israeli school bus with rockets and small arms from the Lebanese side of the frontier (below). The bus was carrying children from the border village of Aviviim. Nine children and three accompanying adults were killed outright and a further twenty children were injured, some seriously (above, one victim on the way to hospital). At the funeral of the victims, Israel's Deputy Premier Allon swore that those responsible for this senseless outrage would receive due punishment.

26th May: When the England World Cup football team stopped off in
Bogotá, the capital of Columbia, on a flight from Quito to Mexico City, they
received a nasty surprise. The England captain *Bobby Moore* was arrested on
suspicion of having stolen a diamond and emerald bracelet from a jewellery
shop a week earlier when England had played a practice match in Bogotá.
As Moore enjoys an irreproachable reputation this smacked of intrigue.
Did the accusation form part of a war of nerves surrounding the World Cup?
The Captain of the World Champions, shown here at a press conference, was
kept under house arrest for three days, until the alleged witnesses made
contradictory statements. He was then released and rejoined his team-mates
in Mexico City, where the England team were in the final stages of preparation
for the 1970 World Cup.

28th May: In the Ceylon general elections Mrs Bandaranaike, leader
of the left-wing coalition, scored a resounding victory over
Prime Minister Dudley Senanayake of the United National Party.
The Governor General *William Gopallawa* (left) called upon *Sirimaro
Bandaranaike* to form a new government. She had formerly ruled
Ceylon between 1960 and 1964, being the world's first woman
Prime Minister. She resumed the left-wing policies which she had
previously followed during her first period of office: nationalisation
and socialisation of the Ceylonese economy, a turn to the Left in
foreign affairs, and the attempt to turn Ceylon from a Commonwealth
state, with Queen Elizabeth II as Head of State, into a republic.

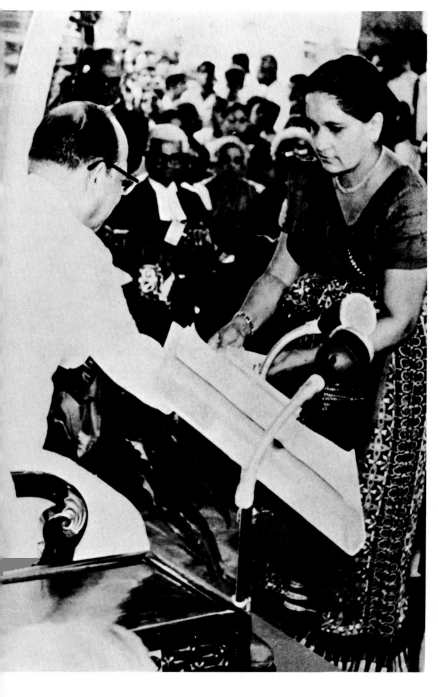

28th May: An attempt by French left-wing extremists to produce a repeat performance of the legendary May Revolution of 1968 failed miserably. The new disorders were spearheaded by Maoist students of the science faculty of the Sorbonne University and of the "Ecole des Beaux-Arts". The riots were sparked off by the dissolution of the left-wing extremist splinter group "La Gauche Prolétarienne" and the conviction of the two editors of the Maoist journal "La Cause du Peuple". Although the students tried out new guerrilla tactics by forming mobile commando groups, they were no match for the riot police during clashes in the Latin Quarter of Paris.

31st May: Peru was afflicted by one of the worst natural disasters of recent decades. A tremor lasting 40 seconds brought catastrophe to an area of 240 km × 130 km in the north of the country, between the port of Chimbote and the ice-clad mountains of the Andes. Nine towns were destroyed, 800,000 Peruvians lost their homes and the death toll stood at around 50,000. In the town of Yungay those who had survived the heavy tremors were subsequently buried by an enormous avalanche of rock, water and mud which crashed down upon the town from Huascaran, Peru's highest mountain (6,766 m), after part of a glacier had fallen into Lake Llanganuco. Where this flourishing city of 21,000 inhabitants had stood before the catastrophe (above), all that now remained was a brownish-yellowish desert of mud (below). The city of Yungay had ceased to exist. Only 500 inhabitants, mainly children attending a matinée performance of a circus with its tent on a hill at the outskirts of the city, survived the holocaust.

June

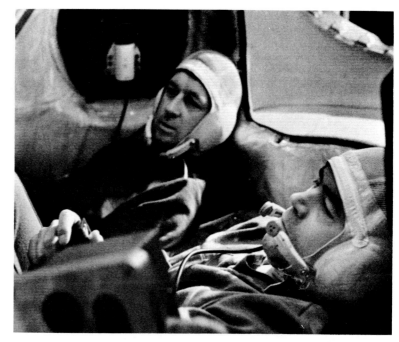

Election sensation in Great Britain:
Tory Leader *Edward Heath* becomes
the new British Prime Minister after
Conservative victory in the General
Election.

New world record in space: the Soyuz 9
cosmonauts *Andrian Nikolayev* (right)
and *Vitali Sevastyanov* orbit the earth
for 17 days, 16 hours and 59 minutes.

For weeks before election day, Harold Wilson, the British Prime Minister, relying on the positive forecasts of all the opinion pollsters, behaved like a man who was confident of winning. While Labour conducted their campaign as a duel between the Prime Minister and the Leader of the Opposition, with the slogan "Who is to lead Britain for the next five years: Wilson or Heath?", the Tory Leader, Edward Heath, facing the possibility of the third successive defeat of his Party, concentrated upon the alarming rise in prices, the trade gap, and the weakness of the pound. By doing this, Heath deprived his opponents of their confidently expected victory. There was a political landslide and the losers, apart from Wilson and the Labour Party, were the opinion pollsters who convinced few by trying to explain away their colossal miscalculation as a shift in attitude during the final phase of the election campaign. There is no doubt that the hitherto unlimited faith in the accuracy of opinion polls suffered a blow of equal seriousness as was dealt them by Harry Truman's sensational victory in the American Presidential Election of 1948, when all the pollsters had forecast his Republican rival Dewey as the winner. But there was a third loser in Britain, the Liberal Party, which was practically eliminated as a political factor from the national scene when they lost over half their seats in Parliament. The trend towards a two-party system became more pronounced and destroyed the Liberals' illusion of being able to establish themselves as a third force in British politics. Wilson failed in his attempt to become the first British politician to win three General Elections in succession.

June 1 Launching of the Soviet spacecraft Soyuz 9 with cosmonauts Andrian Nikolayev and Vitali Sevastyanov.
Argentina's ex-President Pedro Aramburu executed by Peronista underground commandos.

3 First complete synthesis of an artificial gene at the University of Wisconsin.

4 The Pacific kingdom of Tonga achieves independence and becomes 29th member of the British Commonwealth, after being a British Protectorate for 70 years.

8 National crisis in Argentina: President Juan Carlos Ongania deposed by the Armed Forces.

9 Heavy fighting between Jordanian Army and guerrillas. Attempted assassination of King Hussein fails, but the King under pressure of the guerrillas, is forced to dismiss Sherif Nasser bin Jamil, Commander-in-Chief of the Army, and other high-ranking officers.

11 Ehrenfried von Holleben, German Ambassador to Brazil, kidnapped by guerrillas.

14 Brigadier Roberto Levingston proclaimed new President of Argentina.

16 As "ransom" for von Holleben, Brazil agrees to release 40 political prisoners and fly them to Algeria.

17 Von Holleben freed.
Martial law declared in Istanbul after serious disorders.

18 Conservative victory in British General Election.

19 Queen Elizabeth II asks Edward Heath, former Leader of the Opposition, to form a government.
Soft landing of Soyuz 9 in central Siberia after establishing new record in length of orbital flight.

21 Death of former Indonesian President Ahmed Sukarno.

22 Velasco Ibarra, President of Ecuador, assumes dictorial powers.

23 Security pact between United States and Japan extended for one year.

24 Alexander Dubcek relieved of his post as Czechoslovak Ambassador to Turkey.
American attempt at mediation (Rogers Plan) in the Middle East.

25 Heavy fighting between Syria and Israel.

26 Dubcek expelled from the Communist Party of Czechoslovakia.
Arrest of Bernadette Devlin, M.P., sparks off further serious disorders in Ulster.

30 Negotiations start for entry of Britain, Eire, Norway and Denmark into the Common Market.
End of U.S. military operations in the Cambodian border area.

The growing problem of unemployment, the result
of Kenya's rapid progress towards Africanisation,
became increasingly severe. It affected both the Asian
minority, who began a mass exodus from the country,
and the Kenyans. The latter were forced to join long
queues outside employment exchanges. "Troublemakers"
who did not suffer the long hours of waiting with
sufficient patience were roughly handled by the police.
In an unsuccessful attempt to solve the situation by
creating more jobs, President Jomo Kenyatta decreed a
10 per cent increase in the number of employees in the
civil service and the private sector.

1st June: The Russians, 226 days after their triple Soyuz 6, 7 and 8 launch in October 1969, started a new one. They launched into earth orbit the spacecraft Soyuz 9 from the Baikonur cosmodrome in central Asia (the picture shows the spacecraft on top of the rocket shortly before lift-off). The commander of Soyuz 9 was 40-year-old Colonel Andrian Nikolayev, who had travelled into space for the first time in Vostok 3 in 1962. His companion, during the longest and most monotonous human space flight undertaken so far, was Flight Engineer Vitali Sevastyanov, a scientist aged 34 years. The Soyuz 9 cosmonauts did not return to earth until 17 days, 16 hours and 59 minutes had elapsed, thereby considerably improving the record set up by the U.S. Gemini 7 astronauts, Frank Borman and James Lovell, who had spent 13 days, 18 hours and 35 minutes in orbit in December 1965. The scientific experience gained during this record flight was particularly related to the effect of long-term weightlessness on the human organism. During the flight both cosmonauts experienced impairment to their sight and the inability to distinguish between colours. After touchdown, it took them several days to accustom themselves once more to the conditions of gravity on earth. Since the two men had in all other respects come through their test of endurance unscathed, Soviet experts in space medicine gave their opinion that a man could live and work in space for a minimum of one month.

The Soviet authorities showed themselves far more generous with the publication of photographs of the Soyuz 9 mission than with any previous space venture. The picture below shows spacecraft Commander *Nikolayev* and Flight Engineer *Sevastyanov* in their spacious cabin. Being Russians, the two cosmonauts did not miss the chance of establishing a space première: on 9th June they played the first game of chess in space against ground control; it ended in a draw. The world at large, however, was more interested in the lower picture showing the spacecraft after its soft landing in the Kazakhstan steppe, 75 km west of the industrial town of Karaganda. A man has climbed onto the spacecraft in order to open the hatch.

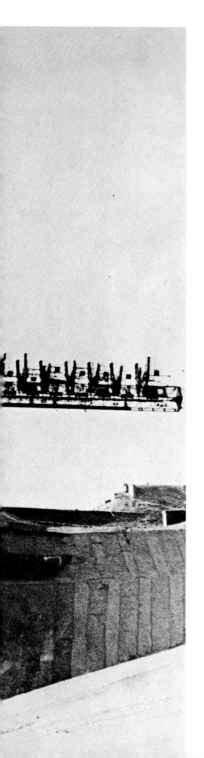

4th June: Involved in a feud with
the authorities over a tax debt of
$471, 49-year-old lorry driver
Arthur Barkley hijacked a TWA
Boeing 727 flying from Phoenix,
Arizona to Washington. Armed
with a pistol, a razor and a can of
petrol, he demanded $100 million
from the U.S. Government as
ransom money for the 51
passengers. The picture, taken by
a passenger, shows Barkley with
pistol in hand standing in the
doorway leading to the cockpit;
next to him is Flight Engineer
Don Salmonson. After the plane
landed at Washington's Dulles
Airport the hijacker was given
$100,000 by TWA. But Barkley
broke his promise to release the
passengers and forced the plane to
refuel and take off for an unknown
destination. Shortly after take-off
he radioed the following "message"
to the President and the Secretary
of State of the U.S.A.: "You are
no good at counting money or at
knowledge of the law." Two and a
half hours later the plane once
more landed at Washington. This
time the FBI took action: they
entered the plane and after a brief
exchange of gun-fire overpowered
the hijacker.

During the second landing, while a pretence was being made of loading sacks full of money which, in fact, contained only scraps of paper, some of the passengers escaped through the emergency exits and took shelter behind a car (picture left). During the exchange of fire the pilot Dale Hupe was injured in the stomach. The hijacker was clearly not responsible for his actions. As he was being taken into custody (picture right), he declared, apparently with reference to his feud with the tax bureau: "If a citizen is not being adequately protected, he has the right to revolt and defend himself."

8th June: The ex-President of France, 78-year-old *Charles de Gaulle*, while holidaying in Spain, was received at the Prado Palace in Madrid by Spain's 77-year-old President *Francisco Franco*, in the presence of Foreign Minister *Gregorio Lopez Bravo*. This was the first time that they had met face to face despite the fact that for decades they had been head of two neighbouring countries. The General and the Generalissimo had a half-hour *tête-à-tête*. De Gaulle who stayed at Cambados, made a number of sightseeing trips, including a visit to Granada and the Alhambra. He was still in Spain for the 30th anniversary of his historic London broadcast to the French people on the 18th June 1940.

Sweden's new Social Democrat Prime Minister *Olof Palme* had a very cool reception on arrival in the United States. The Swedish Government's frank criticism of America's Indo-China policy, the taking up of diplomatic relations with Hanoi and the granting of asylum to some 400 U.S. deserters, had made relations between Washington and Stockholm strained. Attacks on the coloured U.S. Ambassador Jerome Holland by Swedish left-wing radicals had further worsened the mood in Washington. Only a subordinate government official went to greet Palme at the airport. He had talks with Secretary of State Dean Rogers but was not received at the White House. A more understanding attitude was displayed by Senator *William J. Fulbright* (shown in the picture left during a meal with Palme), Chairman of the Senate's Foreign Relations Committee and himself an outspoken critic of American involvement in South-East Asia. A fortnight later Palme met Soviet Prime Minister *Alexei Kosygin* in the restaurant of Moscow's Ostankino television tower, 350m above the ground (below right). The communiqué issued at the end of Palme's Moscow visit showed that there were large areas of agreement between the Swedish Prime Minister and his host in the field of foreign policy. The two successive visits to the capitals of the two great rivals in world affairs made it clear how Palme wanted Sweden's freedom from foreign entanglements to be interpreted abroad: Sweden's neutral attitude was not a neutrality of conviction. A Stockholm newspaper, however, suggested to Palme that he had enjoyed ample opportunities for criticising Washington's Indo-China policies in the U.S.A. but had failed to find an occasion during his Russian visit to censor Brezhnev's attack on Czechoslovakia.

8th June: Within a period of 10 days Argentina experienced the kidnapping and subsequent assassination of one of her most prominent personalities and a change of power in the Casa Rosada in Buenos Aires. The former President, General *Pedro Aramburu* (below right), who had been at the head of the post-Peronist revolutionary government from 1955 to 1958, was abducted from his home by a Peronista underground commando on 29th May, sentenced to death by a "revolutionary tribunal" and executed on 1st June. The sentence of death against the 67-year-old ex-President was justified by his anonymous judges on the grounds of his brutal suppression of the attempted Peronista revolt of 9th June 1956 and subsequent execution of General Juan José Valle, leader of the revolt. Aramburu's corpse had not yet been found when it came to a showdown between President *Juan Carlos Ongania* (left) and the Army who, four years earlier, had helped the cavalry General and Commander-in-Chief of the Army to gain power after the democratically elected President Arturo Illia had been deposed. The 56-year-old President whose authoritarian régime, despite its economic successes, had reached a position of growing isolation after the disorders at Cordoba and Rosario, did not want to adopt the political programme recommended by the military leadership and kept to his "concept of personal authority". Ongania barricaded himself in the Presidential Palace and for 12 hours refused to accept the ultimatum of the Generals. Then he capitulated. His successor, to everybody's surprise, was not the leader of the junta and Commander-in-Chief of the Army, Alejandro Lanusse, but the completely unknown 50-year-old Brigadier *Roberto Marcelo Levingston* (top right) who had made his career in the intelligence service. The call to become Head of State reached him in Washington, where he was the Military Attaché. In his first address to the Argentine people the new President promised a return to constitutional democracy. If Aramburu had not been murdered by his kidnappers, he might well have become the interim President. He had already smoothed the return to democracy once before by installing, against the opposition of his entourage, his elected successor Arturo Frondizi as President.

11th June: Two months after the assassination of Count Spreti by extreme left-wing underground revolutionaries in Guatemala, another German Ambassador was once more in mortal danger in Latin America. Despite being closely guarded by Brazilian security police, Bonn's representative in Rio, 61-year-old *Ehrenfried von Holleben*, was attacked and abducted by a commando of the left-wing underground organisation "Revolutionary People's Vanguard" when returning from the Embassy to his residence in the evening. In the ambush one of von Holleben's guards was shot dead. Chancellor Brandt and Foreign Minister Scheel appealed to the Brazilian Government to do everything possible to save the Ambassador. The guerrillas, who had carried out their action to draw the world's attention to the increasingly repressive measures of the Brazilian military régime, demanded the release of forty political prisoners, who were to be flown to Algeria in return for the German Ambassador. The Government of President Garrastazu Medici surrendered to their demands and released 34 men and 6 women prisoners who were flown to Algeria. After 123 hours in the hands of the guerrillas, Ambassador Holleben was returned to his family and, in front of his residence (picture below), thanked all those who had helped him: "I feel as if I had returned from a long journey".

After the landing of the released prisoners in Algeria the 20-year-old student *Vera Aranjo Magalhaes* had to be carried from the plane. She had been involved in the kidnapping of U.S. Ambassador Elbrick and later badly wounded in an exchange of fire with the police, causing paralysis in both legs.

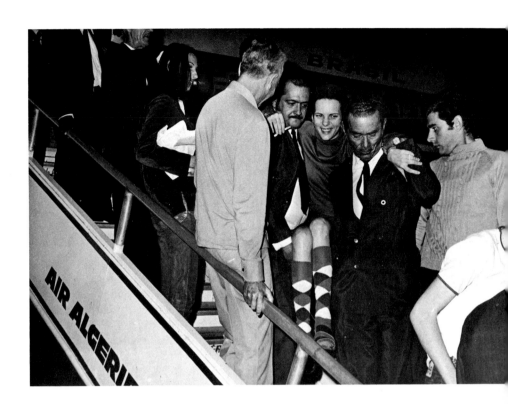

Apolonio de Carvalho, journalist and founder of the "Revolutionary Communist Party of Brazil", acted as spokesman for the group during their first press conference (below). Some of the men and women bore traces of brutal torture.

18th June: Great Britain experienced one of the greatest election surprises of the last few decades. The shock effect of the unexpected success of the Conservative Party in the General Election was similar to the sensational victory of Harry Truman in the American presidential election of 1948. Prime Minister Harold Wilson, relying on the opinion polls, which were recording an unexpectedly rapid rise in the Labour Party's popularity, decided to call a snap General Election. During the campaign the polls, without exception, forecast a clear victory for the Labour Party, despite the fact that Wilson would have been the first Prime Minister in British history to receive the mandate from the electorate to govern three times in succession. Wilson's confident expectation of victory was also based on the prediction by sociologists of a long-term shift towards the Labour Party. In the event, some 30 million British electors decided otherwise. The Tories took 331 of the total of 630 seats, gaining 68 from their opponents. The Labour Party, which lost 61 seats, had to be satisfied with 287. The Liberals, losing half of their strength, returned to the House of Commons with only six M.Ps. Their leader, Jeremy Thorpe, had a margin of only 369 votes in his North Devon constituency. The most surprising defeat was that of *George Brown*, the Deputy Leader of the Labour Party. As a former Foreign Secretary he fought a strenuous campaign on behalf of his Party, touring the country and speaking at as many as five different places in a day (the picture below shows him in Colchester being separated from an opponent by his supporters). Despite his dedication he lost his Belper constituency and after 25 years as an M.P. was barred from the House of Commons. In acknowledgement of his service to the country he was granted a life peerage and took his seat in the House of Lords.

The greatest victor in this General Election held on the 155th anniversary of the Battle of Waterloo was *Edward Heath*, until then Leader of the Opposition. He campaigned on facts and, in defiance of the gloomy forecasts of the pollsters, began his speeches by saying: "I have come to give you a three-word message: we shall win!" Above all, he attacked Wilson's economic policy and criticised the weakness of the pound, the trade gap and the rapid rise in prices. The last of these arguments by the 53-year-old bachelor convinced above all the housewives, like those in Orpington shown here, who played a decisive part in this "shopping basket" election. After the clear-cut victory of the Conservative Party, he was appointed Prime Minister by Queen Elizabeth II.

The handing-over of power was one of those rapid and trouble-free changes typical of the British democratic system. After the Queen had entrusted him with the formation of a new government, *Edward Heath*, the first bachelor for over 60 years to do so, moved into 10 Downing Street (below left) which had been hurriedly vacated by his predecessor. *Harold Wilson* took his departure (below right) calmly: "Such victories are inevitable in a democracy." He promised fair but strong opposition and hinted at his hope to return to 10 Downing Street at a later date. Two days after the election Edward Heath announced his cabinet of 18 ministers.

On their way to attend the solemn opening of Parliament by Queen *Elizabeth II* the new M.Ps. passed the statue of the great British statesman, Sir Winston Churchill. The M.Ps. were headed by the new Prime Minister *Edward Heath* and the new Leader of the Opposition *Harold Wilson*, followed by *Reginald Maudling* the new Home Secretary, and *James Callaghan* his predecessor. The Queen, in her speech from the throne, began by affirming the new government's faith in Europe, and went on to indicate the intention to reconsider the withdrawal from "East of Suez" announced by the Labour Government. However, the strength of the economy and the fight against inflation were underlined as the most important tasks facing the government. The Queen, Prince *Philip*, Prince *Charles* and Princess *Anne* were seated in front of the Peers in traditional regalia during the colourful ceremony.

21st June: Ahmed *Sukarno*, founder and first President of the sixth largest nation in the world, died in an army hospital in Jakarta, aged 69. The father of Indonesia's independence and one of the great leaders of the "Third World" for two decades, he had failed, however, to realise his ambition of creating a synthesis of Nationalism, Marxism and Islam. He died a prisoner of the Army which had never forgiven him the part he played during the attempted Communist insurrection of 30th September 1965. Even though the reputation of the statesman Sukarno had suffered as a result of his policy of confrontation and his mismanagement, his image of a successful lover remained untarnished. Among the women attending his funeral was *Ratna Sari Devi*, his favourite wife, who had hurried from Paris with her young daughter, *Kartika* (centre, below).

22nd June: After two weeks of student disorders and endless quarrels with Parliament, 77-year-old President *José Maria Velasco Ibarra* assumed dictorial powers in Ecuador. He dissolved Congress, suspended the constitution, and closed down the Supreme Court which had declared the raising of new taxes by the President to be unconstitutional. Velasco, who had been five times elected President of the country since 1934 but had only been able to serve one full term, this time enjoyed the full support of the Army which had urged him to remain in office and assume full powers when he declared himself ready to resign.

26th June: Step by step 48-year-old *Alexander Dubcek* had been driven from all positions of responsibility in Prague and Bratislava since the intervention of the Warsaw Pact countries in August 1968. In April 1969 he had to cede his office of Leader of the Communist Party to Gustav Husak; in September of the same year he was expelled from the Party Praesidium; in January 1970 he "voluntarily" resigned from the Central Committee of the Party; and in April he was deprived of his mandate in the Slovak National Assembly. And now the symbolic figure of the Prague Spring was recalled from Turkey, where he was Ambassador (below, left, in Ankara) and two days later expelled by the Central Committee from the Party of which he had been·a member for 31 years. Dubcek had been recalled to Prague to practise self-criticism, but steadfastly refused to retract the political views he had held when in office. It was more than pure coincidence that, at the same time as the almost mystically revered protagonist of "Socialism with a human face" was being turned into "a man of the past", a new bust of Joseph Stalin was unveiled to the Soviet people. It stands over his grave in the wall of the Kremlin (below). Stalinism, which had long been considered dead and buried, was once more rearing its head.

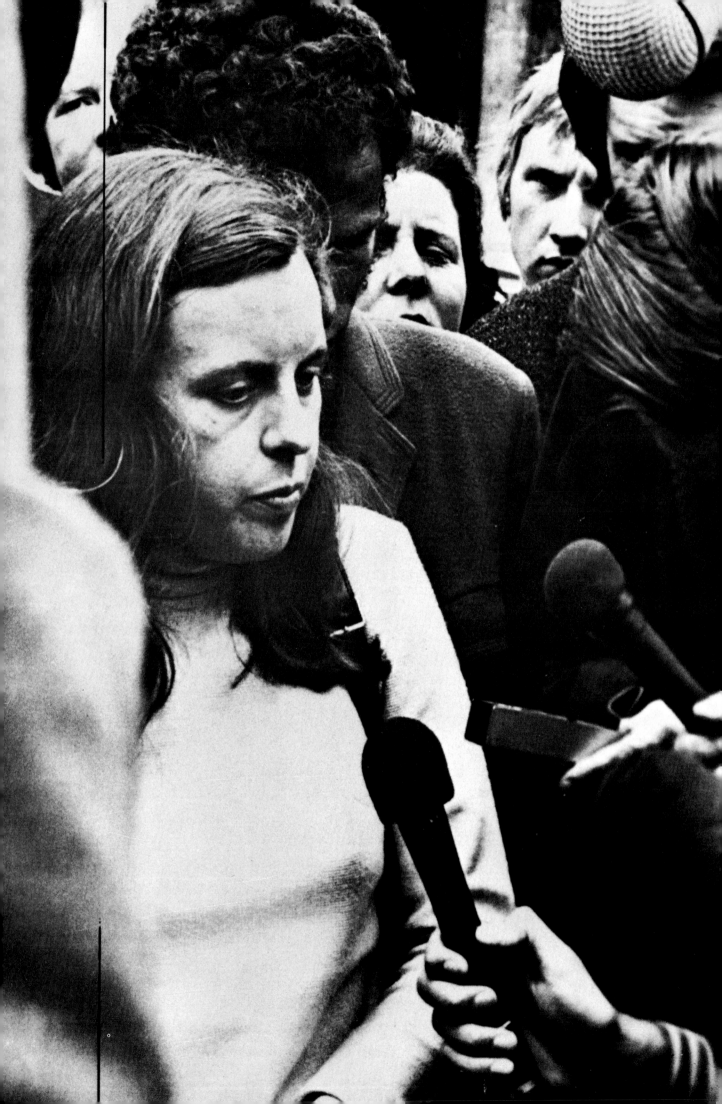

26th June: After weeks of relative calm, the drama in Ulster reached a new climax. The new disorders were sparked off by the arrest of *Bernadette Devlin*, the re-elected young M.P. for Mid-Ulster and civil rights fighter, who had to start a six-month prison sentence after the Belfast Court of Appeal had confirmed the conviction by a Magistrate's Court of riotous behaviour and incitement to riot. The picture left shows Bernadette Devlin giving a final interview before starting her sentence at the women's prison in Armagh. The new government in London had increased the number of troops in Ulster to 11,350 men, but failed to prevent new clashes and more arson. Five civilians were shot dead and more than 200 injured. Sectarian strife even extended to funerals which were the scene of stone-throwing (below right). The Catholic support for civil rights and the Protestant defence of traditional privileges had become merely marginal factors. Street-fighting became routine and violence was practised for the sake of violence. It was the mothers who wanted to put an end to this development and took action. As Catholic youths in Belfast were provoking the soldiers by throwing stones at them, they were suddenly confronted by a living barrier of some 30 women (below left). The confrontation ended when the youths, who did not want to attack their own mothers, quietly dropped their missiles.

In the Le Mans 24-hour sports car race Porsche
gained their first victory in the 47-year-long history
of this strenuous race. This success over the
13·4 km course was the crowning event in the
career of the 42-year-old German racing driver
Hans Herrmann who, together with 30-year-old
Briton Richard Attwood, drove their Porsche 917 to
victory before 400,000 cheering spectators. Only
17 of the 51 super-sports cars finished the race.

The *Daily Mirror* World Cup Rally was the toughest long-distance test in the history of rally driving. It started from London and ended in Mexico City, a distance of 25,000 km, thus linking the venues of the World Cup soccer games of 1966 and 1970. Only 24 out of the 106 cars, with drivers from 19 countries, stayed the course. At the finish of the five-week trial *Hannu Mikkola* of Finland (lower picture with sombero) and co-diver *Gunnar Palm* of Sweden, in a Ford Escort, were the victors by a large margin.

28th June: Some life was injected into French politics by the decision of *Jean-Jacques Servan-Schreiber*, the well-known journalist and author, to take an active part in politics and became a candidate in the Nancy by-election for a seat in the Paris National Assembly. Nancy is in the Lorraine district which is traditionally Gaullist. The government sent five ministers to campaign against Servan-Schreiber, who had resigned as editor of the weekly "L'Express" in order to modernise the Radical Socialist Party as its new Secretary General. He campaigned in Kennedy style and achieved a remarkable victory (above left). He won 55·28 per cent of the votes against a Gaullist and a Communist candidate. The result of the Nancy by-election thus casts a shadow over the next French Presidential Election in 1976.

29th June: The wedding took place at the town hall of Paris-Neuilly of 55-year-old American physician Dr. *Jonas Salk*, who had achieved world fame in 1955 by his discovery of the anti-polio vaccine named after him, and *Françoise Gilot*, who had been Pablo Picasso's companion for many years (above right). Françoise Gilot had achieved world-wide fame when she wrote about her eleven years as model and pupil of the most famous painter of this century, a man forty years her senior, in her book "My Life with Picasso". She met her husband-to-be at a party in La Jolla, California, where Dr. Salk is head of the medical institute.

30th June: Negotiations for the entry of Great Britain, Eire, Norway and Denmark into the Common Market started at the EEC centre in Luxembourg. Thirteen years after the signing of the Treaty of Rome and over seven years after the French veto against British entry, the historic meeting laid the foundation for an enlarged Community. As President of the Council of Ministers of the EEC, Belgium's Foreign Minister Pierre Harmel listed the EEC's conditions for accepting the new candidates: acceptance of the Treaty of Rome and of the decisions taken within the EEC since then, agreement to the ambitious plans for the future (particularly economic and currency union) and acceptance of the political aims enshrined in the preamble to the Treaty. The British delegation made it clear, however, that the new Conservative Government was not prepared to accept membership at any price. The frank, almost tough language did not impair the friendly atmosphere. Even France did not act as killjoy on this occasion: her Foreign Minister *Maurice Schumann* (centre) was in a laughing mood as he witnessed the meeting between Sir *Alec Douglas-Home* (left) and the retiring President of the European Commission, *Jean Rey* of Belgium.

30th June: President Nixon observed the time limit which he had set himself for the search-and-destroy operation in the Cambodian border area. The last American fighting units returned to the points on the other side of the South Vietnamese frontier from where they had launched their attack (the picture shows soldiers of the 199th Infantry Brigade leaving Myron, their base, which they destroyed before their return). Some 30,000 South Vietnamese, however, remained on Cambodian soil. Although the Communists had been driven from their hiding places along the frontier, they remained in control of two-thirds of Cambodia. Despite this, President Nixon called the controversial offensive a resounding success. The Senate did not agree and caused the President the worst defeat in Congress of his career. By a large majority, it condemned the intervention in retrospect and refused Nixon money for any further activity in Cambodia.

July

Pollution of the environment assumes
catastrophic proportions: the fight against
aerial pollution in Tokyo.

This summer the headlines were dominated by a subject totally unconnected with politics, namely the pollution of the environment. All of a sudden, the leading industrial nations became conscious of the fact that the alarming pollution of water, air and soil heralded an imminent environmental catastrophe. The U.S. Senator Thomas J. McIntyre was no longer a lone voice in the wilderness when he declared: "We are in the process of destroying, in the name of progress, the world we are living in." Saving the environment was proclaimed the most important task for the seventies. The fight against the threatened poisoning of the environment advanced to the forefront of domestic politics in the United States. President Nixon proclaimed a "total mobilization" and the most comprehensive programme so far for the protection of the environment. Soviet authorities were equally concerned by the pollution of air and water. Washington and Moscow therefore planned in future to co-operate in this field. A meeting under the auspices of the European Conservation Year in Strasbourg

declared that every European should enjoy the inalienable right to a life which, as far as possible, was to be unpolluted by the waste products of civilization. Even in Japan, a country which has pinned her faith in progress and whose rush to become leader of the industrialized nations has brought almost criminal neglect of the conditions of the environment, there was growing awareness of the dangers and measures were taken to combat the largely invisible threats, such as the poisonous fumes from vehicle exhausts. What was visible were the layers of smog above the closely built-up areas, the rivers transformed into stinking sewers, and the dying lakes. The world-wide struggle against environmental pollution, with its dangers of disease and death, will create economic and social problems. To ameliorate the situation by applying technological methods to preserve the environment will require enormous sums of money. The prime objective of the sixties was to place a man on the moon. The objective of the current decade is to enable man to exist on an unpolluted earth.

July 2 President Nixon appoints Ambassador David Bruce as new Vietnam Chief Negotiator in Paris.

3 France explodes her second hydrogen bomb on the Mururoa atoll in the South Pacific.

5 The government candidate Luis Echevarria wins the presidential election in Mexico.
President Sihanouk of Cambodia sentenced to death in his absence by a military tribunal in Phnom Penh.
The Queen, Prince Philip and Princess Anne start 10-day tour of the N.W. Territories of Canada.

6 The Rumor government in Italy resigns.
New Soviet-Roumanian friendship and assistance treaty signed in Bucharest.

10 Iceland's Prime Minister Bjarne Benediktsson killed in fire.

11 Commonwealth Games open in Edinburgh.

12 Successful Atlantic crossing by Thor Heyerdal in the papyrus boat "Ra II".

14 Ahti Karjalainen forms new Finnish Government.

16 Dock strike in Great Britain. The Government declares state of emergency.
The corpse of assassinated ex-President Aramburu of Argentina found in Carlos Tejedor.
Disorders in Reggio di Calabria after Catanzaro has been chosen as regional capital.

20 Norwegian liner "Fulvia" founders near Canary Islands after fire aboard: all crew and passengers safe.
Britain's Chancellor of the Exchequer Ian Macleod dies suddenly, aged 56.

21 Finnish Major-General Ensio Siilasvuo succeeds Odd Bull as Head of the U.N. Armstice Commission for the Far East.

22 Greek Government accepts ultimatum by Arab hijackers after the abduction of a plane: seven terrorists to be released within a month.

23 President Nasser accepts the American "Rogers" peace plan for the Middle East.
Coup d'état in Muscat and Oman: Sultan Said bin Taimur deposed by his son Qabus.

27 Start of German-Soviet negotiations between Foreign Ministers Scheel and Gromyko in Moscow.
Death of 81-year-old former Portuguese Prime Minister Antonio Salazar.
In Cuba Dr Castro admits economic setbacks and rhetorically offers to resign.

28 Soviet Union launches test model of nuclear space bomb into earth orbit.
Cairo closes down radio stations run by Palestine guerrillas in opposition to the "Rogers" peace plan.
Anthony Barber (50) appointed as Britain's new Chancellor of the Exchequer.

29 End of British dock strike.
Death of 70-year-old Sir John Barbirolli, conductor of the Hallé Orchestra for 25 years.

30 Brigadier Andrew Juxon-Smith, former military dictator of Sierra Leone, sentenced to death.

31 Israel accepts U.S. peace plan.

Jack Hayward, a businessman, put up £150,000 to pay for the salvaging of Brunel's 3,300-ton ocean-going masterpiece, *Great Britain*, the first propeller driven iron steamship, which had been abandoned in the Falkland Islands in 1886. The epic tow across the Atlantic ended when the ship reached Bristol on 5th July, where she had been launched 127 years previously. The picture shows her passing under the famous Avon suspension bridge, which was also designed by Brunel. It is intended to restore the ship and to find a home for her, possibly near the Tower of London.

6th July: Dr Patrick Hillery, Minister for External Affairs in the Irish Republic (right), disclosed that he had paid a secret visit to the Falls Road area of Belfast, Northern Ireland, at the request of the Prime Minister of the Republic of Ireland, Jack Lynch. The purpose was to "relax tension". The personal visit had been made without the normal notification to the authorities in Northern Ireland, usually made as a matter of courtesy. Dr Hillery's disclosure caused the British Government considerable embarrassment, and was regarded by Ulster Unionists as an unwarranted intrusion at a difficult time. The Republic believes that "provocative" parades should be banned in Ulster. Major Chichester-Clark, Northern Ireland's Prime Minister, said he would be greatly relieved if the Orange marches organized for 13th July were called off; but he would "probably" be joining an Orange march himself.

7th July: Reports by Congressmen Augustus Hawkins and William Anderson of the conditions on the South Vietnamese prison island of Con Son, 230 km south-east of Saigon, caused a sensation in the United States and indignation in the rest of the world. Some 500 political prisoners were locked up in "tiger cages" in Camp 4 of this South Vietnamese "Devil's Island" (above left), populated by 10,000 convicts. Men and women were chained to the floor in narrow, damp and dirty cages, one next to the other, without doors or windows. The only way to look into them was from above, through iron bars (above). The cages (below left) had been built as torture chambers during the sixties of the last century. "It was the most shocking treatment of human beings that we have ever seen", declared Anderson. Most of the political prisoners had been banished to the island without a trial. They were starving, thin as skeletons, sick and without medical care. If they complained, a warder threw unslaked lime over them. After the sickening disclosures about the degrading conditions on Con Son, the Saigon Government stated that "the tiger cages were no longer suitable for housing prisoners" and had the 500 inmates flown back to Saigon.

149

10th July: The People's Republic of China prematurely released the American Bishop, *James Edward Walsh*, because of his age and his bad health. He had been sentenced in Shanghai to 20 years' imprisonment for alleged espionage in 1958. In Rome, where he had an audience with Pope Paul, the 79-year-old missionary criticized the curtailment of freedom by the Chinese régime, but praised some of the Communist government's reforms as "very useful and beneficial". He particularly stressed three reforms which "represent a magnificent constructive advance for the Chinese people": the end of discrimination against women and against different races, and the absolute prohibition of immorality and indecency in public and in the theatre. He added that even in prison he had been able to notice signs of the healthy spirit prevailing in China.

Before the scars of the civil war had been able to heal, the Yemen, an economically and socially retarded country, was afflicted by a new disaster. Large parts of the country were affected by famine, resulting from the lack of rain during the past three years. This extremely long drought threatened a million Yemenis with death by starvation. Most of them would have been doomed without international aid. Medical care was quite inadequate, as there are only seventy doctors for the whole country. The picture shows a heavily veiled woman in Ta'iz bringing her dying child to the only children's hospital in the country, which is maintained by a Swedish children's charity.

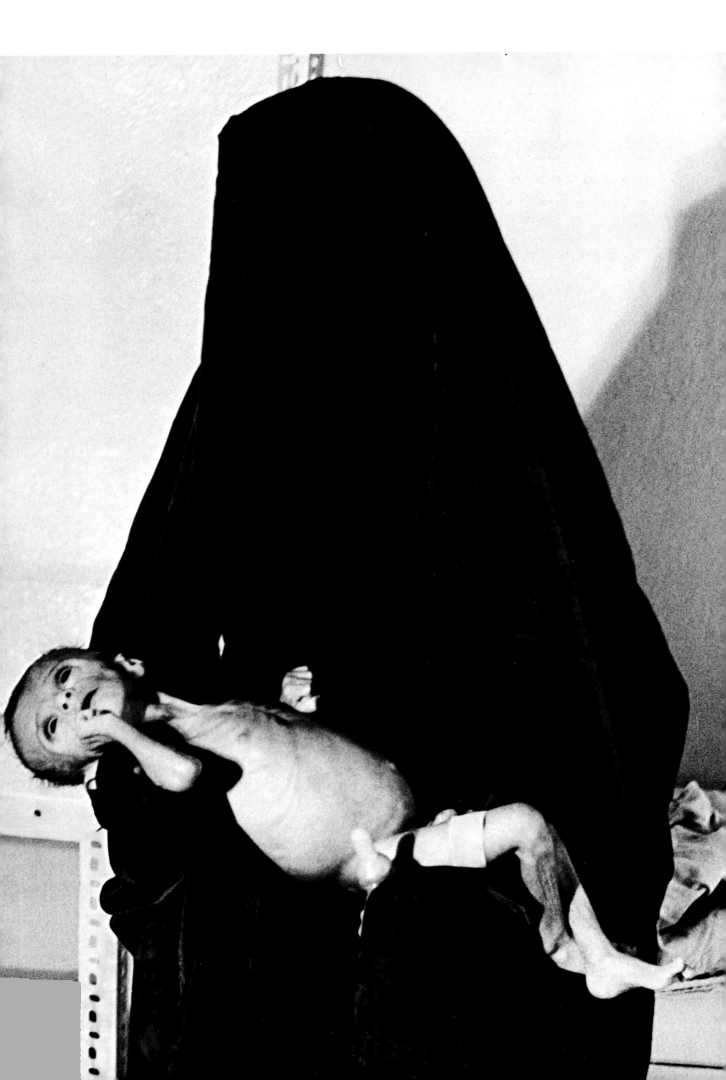

12th July: After the Norwegian explorer and anthropologist *Thor Heyerdal* had failed in his first attempt to cross the Atlantic in a papyrus boat, the second voyage was crowned with success. In the previous year "Ra I" had sunk in heavy seas shortly before reaching its destination. But this time "Ra II", which set sail from the port of Safi in Morocco with an international crew of eight on 17th May, successfully reached Bridgetown, in Barbados, two months later. 55-year-old bearded Heyerdal, shown in the picture left being mobbed by admirers, ascribed part of the success of his second attempt to the fact that "Ra II" had been built by South American Indians from the area of Lake Titicaca, while "Ra I" had been made from papyrus bushes by Africans. The design of the boat was based on ancient friezes in Egyptian tombs; the purpose of the 5150-km journey was to prove that the peoples of the Mediterranean region had been able to cross the Atlantic in such boats thousands of years ago and thus carry their civilization into the "New World". Heyerdal also made a discovery concerning modern civilization: that the Atlantic was polluted by oil "from horizon to horizon", which he duly reported to U Thant, the U.N. Secretary-General.

12th July: Marisol Malaret Contreras, a 20-year-old secretary from Puerto Rico, was chosen Miss Universe 1970 at Miami Beach and crowned by her Brazilian predecessor *Gloria Diaz* (left). The beauty queen from Puerto Nuevo with dark hair and green eyes is an orphan. With the title she won $10,000 in cash, a similar amount for various representative duties, furs worth $6,500, and clothes for one year. Asked, during an interview, to name the greatest man alive, she had no hesitation in choosing Wernher von Braun, the German-American rocket designer.

14th July: Mobile missile-launching apparatus and other vehicles of the "Force de frappe" were shown for the first time in France during the traditional military parade on their national day. President Pompidou took the salute at the march past of 10,000 soldiers, 650 vehicles and 165 planes and helicopters. Against the imposing backdrop of the Arc de Triomphe, missile transporters with their egg-shaped containers used for carrying nuclear warheads, formed part of the parade moving along the Champs Élysées. However, the strategic medium-distance rockets with a range of 3000 km, which belong to the same series of weapons, were not on show.

16th July: The new Conservative Government in Britain reacted with great calmness and success to the first major labour dispute of its term in office, possibly in the hope that the need for legislation to reform industrial relations would be underlined. The outbreak of the first country-wide dock strike since 1926, endangering supplies and paralysing exports, was met with the declaration of a state of emergency. There was not, however, any premature recourse to the use of troops in the forty British ports abandoned by the 47,000 dockers, even though the strike threatened to affect the balance of payments (the picture left shows the desolate scene in the strike-bound Royal Albert Docks in London). After the strike had lasted for a fortnight, the leaders of the Transport and General Workers' Union reached an agreement with the employers which guaranteed the dockers a wage rise of approximately 7 per cent, so giving them a weekly minimum wage of £20. This failed to satisfy the more militant strikers, who booed the union leaders (above). But the hardliners, who had forced the country-wide strike against the wishes of the Union officials by wild-cat strikes, were in a minority, and work in the ports was resumed.

16th July: The Italian Government's decision to decentralize the administration of the country by the formation of Regions had unexpected consequences. First the Adriatic port of Pescara was the scene of several days of protest by its inhabitants against the choice of her rival, L'Aquila, as provincial capital. Then there were disorders, lasting several weeks, in Reggio at the southern tip of Italy, after the considerably smaller town of Catanzaro had been selected as the seat of the administration for the newly-formed region of Calabria. The indignation felt by the people of Reggio sparked off violent street fighting and bomb outrages in this economically underprivileged south Italian port, leading to several deaths, hundreds of injured, and widespread damage to property. The government sent in large detachments of police to deal with the revolutionary situation in the city, which was periodically racked by general strikes, but even this measure failed to bring the situation under control. When the demonstrators disrupted rail traffic and blocked the roads, the government brought in troops, but the situation did not improve until the new Prime Minister, Emilio Colombo, promised economic aid to the rebellious region.

27th July: Aged 81 years, the former Portuguese Prime Minister *Antonio de Oliveira Salazar* (left) died in Lisbon after a long illness. From 1932 until September 1968 he had ruled Portugal as a dictator. It was in 1928 that as a Professor of Economics in the provincial town of Coimbra, he was summoned to Lisbon to restore the financial situation of the country. Four years later, after he had completed this mission, President Carmona appointed him Head of the Government. Salazar coined the phrase "new state", which was intended to make the Portuguese conscious of their one-time greatness through the symbol of national unity. However, this devout ascetic, who never wore decorations or uniform, reduced his "new state" to stagnation and turned Portugal into the last classic colonial power in Europe. When he was half-paralysed by a stroke and his life was ebbing away no one had the courage to tell him that he was no longer at the helm. His passing came as a relief. Nevertheless, people lined the railway track (below) all along the 200-km route, from Lisbon to his native village of Santa Comba Dao, to pay their last respects, as a special train carried his remains which, according to his wish, were to be interred in a simple grave.

In the course of this summer, the authorities in New York and Tokyo were forced ever more frequently to sound the smog alarm. The clouds of haze hovering above the large conurbations became an everyday phenomenon, and aerial pollution reached dangerous proportions. During a single day, hundreds of people in Tokyo visited hospitals with bronchial trouble and inflammation of the eyes. Doctors pilloried the alarming aerial pollution as one of the factors in the increase of coronary and circulatory diseases, and of cancer. The oily, yellowish fog over the cities allowed heat to penetrate, but almost completely shut out the sunlight. In New York, the build up of heat beneath the layer of fog (above) caused an additional crisis when the inhabitants, in order to cope with the stifling heat, turned up the air conditioning as far as possible. The resulting rise in electricity consumption threatened to cause a breakdown, and the subway was only able to move at snail's pace. Mayor Lindsay was forced to invoke a state of emergency to enable him to apply drastic measures to the smog situation. In Japan Prime Minister Sato created a central body to combat environmental pollution, headed by himself. Until then he had always supported the view of the large industries that any measure taken to preserve the environment was bound to harm economic expansion.

Smoke, soot, exhaust fumes and noisome smells trouble the inhabitants of many industrial areas: the smoking chimneys of Vargön darken the Swedish sky.

Australia was also affected by aerial pollution: the picture shows smog over Sydney with its two million inhabitants. Aerial pollution is now an international problem.

The Japanese children of Yokkaichi, where 40 per cent of all inhabitants are suffering from bronchial disease, are compelled to wear gauze masks on their way to school: ruthless exploitation of natural resources by a society, which has turned technical progress into a fetish, has caused disastrous side-effects upon its own environment.

It used to be the custom for both younger and older women to accept the edict of the Paris fashion moguls without resistance at the start of each new season. This year, however, they have rebelled against the decision to banish the mini and relegate it to fashion history. In this resistance against the fashion designers they enjoyed the support of many men, who were enthusiastically in favour of the mini fashion, even though their motives were largely selfish. But whether it was only a mini-demonstration for the mini, as here in Munich, or a large-scale demonstration against the maxi fashion, they were rearguard actions. Even if the "Long Look", and, by way of compromise the midi, were introduced against considerable opposition, the trend clearly favoured a marked drop in hemlines. And this despite the fact that mini fans, looking forward to the next summer, alleged that young girls were apt to look like prematurely aged grandmothers.

August

Under pressure from Washington and Moscow, Israel and Egypt accept the "Rogers" peace plan: cease-fire along the Suez Canal. Tactical feint or genuine desire for peace?

The Second World War is forgotten: Federal Chancellor *Willy Brandt* and Party Leader *Leonid Brezhnev* seen together after putting their signatures to the treaty between Russia and West Germany providing for co-operation and the renunciation of force. "Perhaps an historic moment," said the Soviet leader . . .

Thirteen months after President Nasser had denounced the 1967 armistice and proclaimed a war to "grind down" Israel, the peace plan of U.S. Secretary of State Rogers became the basis of a cease-fire. Before the "Rogers" plan was accepted, there was violent controversy among the Arabs as well as among the Israelis. Because of his more conciliatory attitude, Nasser was accused by the Palestine guerrillas, supported by Baghdad and Algiers, of "conspiring with U.S. imperialists". Golda Meir had to pay for her reluctant agreement to the plan by a crisis affecting her coalition government, since the right-wing Gahal party considered Nasser's acceptance as a mere tactical feint and resigned from the government in protest against a "Middle East Munich". The cautious optimism, which considered a political solution of the Middle East conflict a possibility, soon suffered a considerable setback. Shortly after the start of the peace talks, the Jarring mission, which was to mediate between the Arabs and Israelis, was boycotted by the Israelis, because the United Arab Republic, in contravention of the cease-fire agreement, had strongly reinforced its missile belt along the Suez Canal.

For the first time since 1955, when Konrad Adenauer agreed to the resumption of diplomatic relations with the then Communist leaders, Khrushchev and Bulganin, in Moscow, and had obtained the return of all German prisoners of war in the Soviet Union as a quid pro quo, a Federal German Chancellor visited Moscow. Willy Brandt went to sign the Russo-German treaty on co-operation and the renunciation of force. By appending his signature Brandt acknowledged the European realities brought about by the Second World War, and the prevailing Soviet sphere of power. At the same time, however, he removed the largest obstacle in the way of normalizing relations with the other states of the Communist block. Moscow, on the other hand, was interested in an improvement of the political climate after 25 years of confrontation with Bonn for mainly economic reasons. A military superpower, but economically in many respects still a developing country, Communist Russia needs closer economic and technical co-operation with the highly developed capitalist Germany in order not to be left behind completely in the race with the U.S.A. Exaggerated concern in the West, which invoked the ghost of Rapallo, was soothed by Brandt who emphasized that the free society of the Federal Republic was strongly anchored in its alliance to the West.

August 4 Israel agrees to the "Rogers" peace plan. Gahal Ministers resign from the Meir Government.

5 Iraq and Algeria boycott the Arab conference at Tripoli.

6 Emilio Colombo forms the 32nd Italian postwar Government.

7 Cease-fire between Israel and the United Arab Republic/Jordan.

9 U.S. police adviser Dan Mitrione murdered by Tupamaros in Montevideo: civil rights in Uruguay suspended for twenty days.

12 Brandt and Kosygin sign Russo-German treaty in Moscow.

13 Israel demands withdrawal of Egyptian missiles from standstill zone along Suez Canal. Greece releases seven Arab terrorists.

14 Second round of SALT talks in Vienna end.

17 Suleiman Franjieh elected President of the Lebanon.

18 Controversial dumping of nerve gas rockets off the coast of Florida.

19 Communist block summit meeting in Moscow.

22 U.S. Vice-President Agnew leaves for trip to Asia.

24 Emperor Haile Selassie opens conference of the Organization of African Unity at Addis Ababa. Britain's proposed sale of arms to South Africa condemned.

25 Indirect Middle East peace talks led by Gunnar Jarring start in New York.

28 Palestine National Council sitting in Amman completely rejects "Rogers" plan.

29 Clashes in Amman between Jordanian Army and guerrillas.

31 Ambonese occupy Indonesian Embassy in The Hague and kill policeman. Nobel Prizewinner François Mauriac dies aged 85.

3rd August:
America's new Poseidon missile was successfully fired from underwater for the first time—and in the presence of Soviet observers. As the two-stage missile, fired from the nuclear submarine "James Madison" at a depth of 40 m, was rising from the Atlantic near Cape Kennedy with its fuel igniting just above the surface of the water (picture), the Soviet spy ship "Laptev", equipped with sophisticated electronic equipment, was so intent upon recovering floating debris of the starting mechanism that it almost collided with a U.S. destroyer. During the mutual protests the second stage of the Poseidon covered the full distance of some 4600 km to its target area in the Atlantic.

6th August: Twenty-five years ago, at 8.15 a.m., the U.S. B-29 bomber "Enola Gay", on the orders of President Truman, dropped the first atom bomb, called "Little Boy" and weighing 4500 kg, on an enemy target. This target was the Japanese city of Hiroshima, inhabited by 440,000 people, which has since become the universal symbol of the horror of nuclear war and of the gigantic destructive power of mankind. On the 25th anniversary of the explosion 50,000 people remembered the victims of the cataclysm in Hiroshima, once more a flourishing city. The mayor unveiled a commemorative stone engraved with the names of 3,606 Japanese whose deaths during the previous year were the result of the delayed effects of the nuclear explosion. Despite this lingering sickness, however, the horror of nuclear death has finally been relegated to the realm of history in Japan. The picture of the fiery mushroom, in Hiroshima's atomic museum, serves as a memorial to that tragic day of 6th August, 1945, when the name of Hiroshima was engraved upon the history of the human race.

7th August: Pressure by Washington and Moscow led to a cease-fire along the 160-km long Suez front, based on an initiative by U.S. Secretary of State William Rogers. His Middle East plan, which was initially to last for ninety days, and provided for the revival of the Jarring mission, caused violent controversy in both camps. The Palestine guerrillas, supported by Baghdad and Algiers, indignantly rejected any peaceful solution of the Middle East conflict and called President Nasser a traitor. In Israel the coalition of national unity, formed on the eve of the Six-day War of June 1967, broke up when the right-wing Gahal Party, in protest against the "neglect of national interests", withdrew its six Ministers from the Government. The majority on both sides, however, welcomed the cease-fire: the Egyptians were tired of carrying the main burden of the fight against Israel, and the Israelis had observed with mounting concern the growing involvement of Moscow in Arab affairs. Flights by Soviet pilots over Egypt had threatened to lead to a direct confrontation with the Soviet Union. The hopes created by the cease-fire were soon disappointed, since the Egyptians profited from the lull in the fighting to extend their missile sites along the Canal. Although the Israeli soldiers were able to continue their peaceful activities in their positions (above), the Government in Jerusalem refused to open peace talks until the Sam 2 and Sam 3 missiles, installed in the standstill zone in violation of the agreement, had been withdrawn. This caused considerable ill-feeling between Washington and Jerusalem, since the United States, who had guaranteed Israel an unchanged military *status quo* during the cease-fire, dragged its feet when it came to accusing Nasser of violating the cease-fire agreement. Prime Minister *Golda Meir* flew to Washington in order to convince President *Richard Nixon* that her Government was not prepared to accept peace at any price (left).

Two court cases hit the headlines in the United States. The first, a minor drug offence, would hardly have attracted attention, had it not been for the fact that one of the Kennedy family was involved. 16-year-old *Robert Kennedy Jnr.*, second eldest son of the murdered Senator, and Sargent Shriver Jnr., his cousin, appeared in a juvenile court at Barnstable, Mass., charged with the illegal possession of marijuana. He was accompanied by his mother, *Ethel*, and his uncle, Senator *Edward Kennedy*. The judge said that the charges would be dismissed after a period of probation of one year.

The second case in the courthouse at San Rafael in California was the scene of a dramatic attempt to set a prisoner free, which caused the death of four people. During the trial of 37-year-old *James McClain* (a coloured man accused of having attacked a warder at the nearby San Quentin penitentiary with a kitchen knife), a 17-year-old negro Jonathan Jackson suddenly stood up in the spectators' gallery, threatened the court with a gun and threw a pistol to the accused. Although he was wearing handcuffs, McClain succeeded in catching the pistol and pointed it at the head of 65-year-old Judge *Harold Haley*. The Judge, threatened with instant death, ordered the shackles to be removed from McClain. The two negroes then liberated another two coloured prisoners, who were attending as witnesses. *William Christmas* forced the jurors *Joyce Rodoni, Doris Wittmer* and *Maria Graham*, as well as 32-year-old

prosecuting attorney *Gary Thomas* towards the lift as hostages (left), while McClain pushed the Judge, to whose neck he had attached a sawn-off automatic with adhesive tape, into a van which Jackson had parked in front of the building (above). The area in front of the courthouse was surrounded by about a hundred police and prison warders, who had been alerted whilst on a nearby shooting range and had blocked the exit with two cars. When, despite this, the gangsters tried to make their escape, they came under concentrated fire. McClain, Christmas and Jackson were shot dead. Judge Haley, shot in the head by the gun suspended round his neck, was also killed. Prosecuting attorney Thomas, whose spine was crushed by a bullet, was paralysed for life. Before the shooting started the criminals had called to press photographer, Jim Kean: "You take pictures of anything you like. We are revolutionaries."

12th August: Thirty-one years after the conclusion of the Hitler-Stalin pact in 1939, which was followed by four years of fighting and 25 years cold war, Federal German Chancellor *Willy Brandt* and Soviet Premier *Alexei Kosygin*, in the presence of Party Leader *Leonid Brezhnev* in the Kremlin, signed the Russo-German treaty renouncing force and providing for co-operation. During the solemn ceremony the two Heads of Government were flanked by their Foreign Ministers, Walter Scheel (hidden) and *Andrei Gromyko*, who had initialled the treaty on the 7th August, after eleven days of difficult negotiations. Next to Brezhnev stood the West German State Secretary *Egon Bahr*, the real architect of the agreement, the outline of which he had determined during seven months of talks with Gromyko. After the signing ceremony Brandt had a four-hour private talk with Brezhnev. The main subject was the Berlin problem. Brandt, who had previously emphasized that ratification of the treaty by the German Bundestag was dependent upon progress in the four-power talks on Berlin, drew Brezhnev's attention to the vital interest of the Federal Republic of Germany in safeguarding the links and communications between West Germany and Berlin. In a televised speech transmitted from Moscow to West Germany the Chancellor characterized the agreement as a success for German post-war policies. He said, "the treaty did not concede anything which had not long since been lost already. We have the courage to turn a new leaf in history." The success of the SPD/FDP coalition in negotiating the biggest step forward in the field of foreign policy since World War II had thrown into confusion the CDU/CSU opposition, who voiced serious reservations about the treaty. According to them, it did not represent a new start; rather, by surrendering positions of freedom and abandoning national interests, it amounted to making concessions without gaining anything in return.

Despite many recent pronouncements that the time of large-scale pop festivals was over, hundreds of thousands of pop fans and hippies gathered on a 17-hectare site in the Isle of Wight for a "festival of love". Only the organizers, who invested £500,000 in the festival, were disappointed. They lost a large amount of the expected takings, when tens of thousands camped on the surrounding hills outside the fenced-in arena and enjoyed the music without paying, thanks to the powerful amplifying equipment.

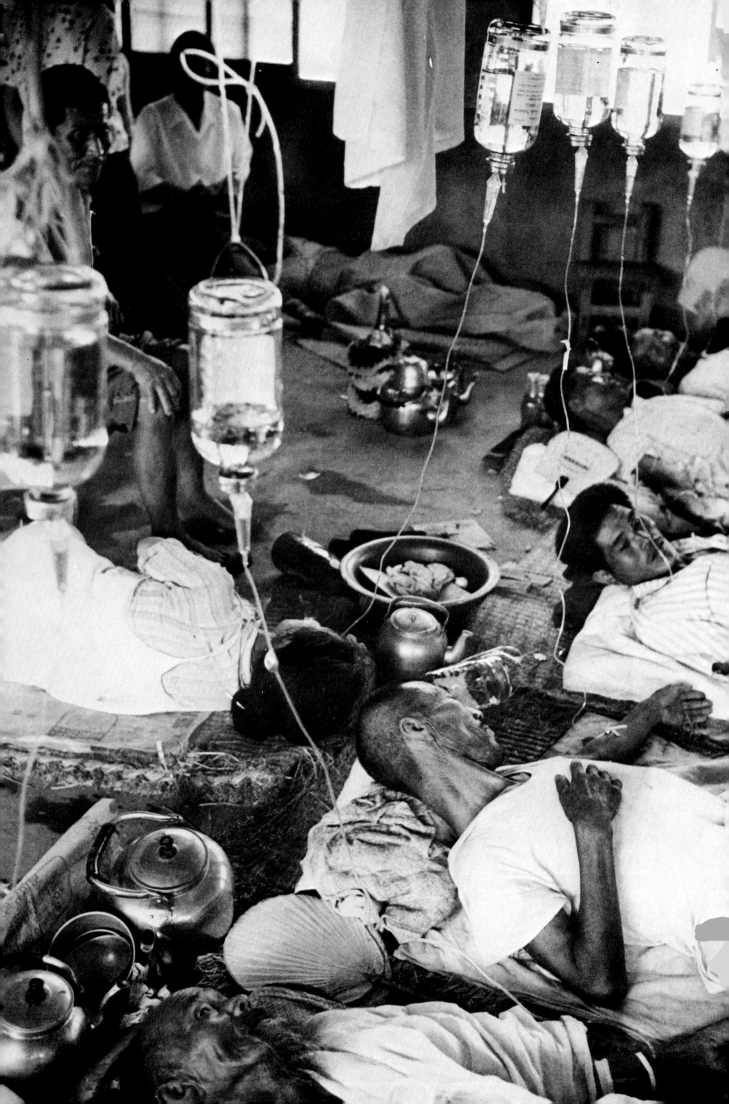

For the first time since 1923 an epidemic of cholera broke out in Europe and spread to several other areas in the world. Because of its infectiousness and brief incubation period the disease is extremely difficult to combat. The epidemic penetrated as far as southern Russia, where several cities had to be sealed off from the rest of the country. It also advanced into Czechoslovakia where a number of fatal cases were reported. Despite extensive precautionary measures and mass inoculations, the progress of the disease through the Middle East failed to be halted at the borders of Israel and Turkey. The El Tor variety of the virus (a variant of the classic cholera virus) also broke out in several West African countries and in the Far East. In South Korea so many people were infected that, as shown in the picture of Changnyong on the left, schools had to be turned into emergency hospitals, and patients lay on the floor to receive serum by drip-feed. Since the discovery of the cholera virus by the bacteriologist Robert Kock of Germany, 83 years ago, the disease has been confined to the underdeveloped countries of the world.

18th August: Violent protests were made against the decision by the American army to dump more than 12,000 obsolete rockets containing the deadly nerve gas GB in the Atlantic. It was feared that the 410 "coffins", made of reinforced concrete and holding the containers filled with the poisonous gas, which originated from the U.S. arsenal at Richmond, Kentucky (top picture), might be unable to withstand the unknown pressures and sea currents. After the legal steps taken by the Governor of Florida to stop the plan had been defeated, the ancient Liberty ship "Le Baron Russell Briggs" with the 67-ton cargo was scuttled (above) 450 km off the coast of Florida, where the wreck with its deadly cargo now rests at a depth of 5000 m.

20th August: The submarine fleet of the French Navy continued its run of bad luck. Only five months after the loss of the "Euridyce", the "Galatée", also of the Daphne class, collided with the "Maria van Riebeek", her sister ship built for South Africa, during an underwater mission off Toulon. Six members of the crew of the "Galatée" were killed. The "Maria van Riebeek" was able to reach Toulon harbour but the "Galatée", badly damaged by an explosion, had to be beached in order to avoid a worse disaster. Recovery and repair vessels hastened to the assistance of the damaged submarine, resting on a pebble beach at the foot of some cliffs. Only the bows and a part of the conning tower were showing above the water (picture). Since the end of the war France has lost five submarines, with a death toll of 183 sailors.

25th August: After the cease-fire along the Suez front had come into force, more than two weeks elapsed before the indirect peace talks between the United Arab Republic, Jordan and Israel, under the aegis of *Gunnar Jarring*, active as U.N. mediator since 1967, got off the ground. Agreement on the venue and level of negotiations was reached only with difficulty. While the Arabs wanted to hold the talks at ambassadorial level at the United Nations in New York, the Israelis would have preferred talks between Foreign Ministers away from New York. In the end Israel gave way and the talks were started, in accordance with the "Rhodes formula" (applied by U.N. diplomat Ralph Bunche to bring about an armistice in the Middle East in 1949), between the Ambassadors of the three countries until the positions of both sides had been clarified, in preparation for possible negotiations at Foreign Minister level. For the time being, however, this objective was not reached, since the Israeli Government in protest against Egyptian cease-fire violations, blocked the Jarring mission soon after the beginning of the talks, declaring that it was prepared to return to the conference table only after the Egyptians had withdrawn the missiles which, in contravention of the agreement, they had positioned in the standstill zone. Since the Egyptians made no attempt to fulfil this condition but continued to reinforce their defence system against aerial attack, the Swedish diplomat (above) once more packed his bags and left New York to resume his post as Ambassador in Moscow.

26th August: Fifty years after American women had gained the right to vote, militant campaigners for women's rights once more took to the streets of the United States in order to demonstrate for complete equality of the two sexes in education, work and society, and against the sexual abuse of women. To emphasize their demands the leaders of the women's liberation movement "NOW" issued a call to all American women to join a nation-wide general strike in homes and offices. Although attracting a lot of publicity they were unable to prevent the demonstrations for women's rights from turning into carnival-like processions in many places.

31st August: The first state visit by an Indonesian President to the Netherlands took place under unfavourable conditions. On the eve of the arrival of General *Suharto* a group of heavily armed young Ambonese stormed the Indonesian Embassy at Wassenaar near The Hague, shot a policeman dead, and held members of the family and staff of the Ambassador, who managed to escape, as hostages for several hours. It was only when J. A. Manusama, recognized by the exiled Ambonese as President of the "Republic of the South Moluccas" (proclaimed in 1960), intervened that the 36 insurgents surrendered to the Dutch police (the picture left shows one of the armed intruders in the garden of the Embassy). The Ambonese had carried out their spectacular action to force a meeting between Manusama and Suharto. These circumstances caused Suharto's state visit to be curtailed to a single day. The picture right shows the Indonesian President with Queen *Juliana,* his hostess, who welcomed him on his arrival at the Ypenburg air force base and accompanied him on the last part of his journey by helicopter.

31st August: The death occurred in Paris of the celebrated French writer François Mauriac, at the age of 85. He is considered one of the most important Catholic novelists of our time. Since 1933 he had been a Member of the Académie Française; and in 1952 he was awarded the Nobel Prize for literature for the "penetrating psychological and artistic intensity" with which he interpreted the human drama. The descendant of a rich and strict Christian family, he first made his name as a poet in 1909. His first big success was the novel "Le Baiser au lépreux" in 1922. Although he had become a towering figure during his lifetime, Mauriac was not the type to shut himself off from the world. Right up to his last days he involved himself as a journalist with questions of French and international politics, often in conflict with his class and his Church.

September

The wave of hijackings by political provocateurs escalates: the giant jets of Swissair, TWA and BOAC ablaze at the "Airport of the Revolution", in the North Jordanian desert after being blown up by "Popular Front" guerrillas.

Egypt's President *Gamal Abdel Nasser*, the man who dominated the scene in the Middle East for two decades, dies.

After a bloody civil war, King *Hussein* of Jordan makes another political compromise with the Palestine guerrillas.

September was a particularly eventful month in the Middle East, where tension had lessened to some extent after the cease-fire along the Suez Canal. If it had not been for international intervention, the area east of the Nile might easily have become the scene of an international conflict with disastrous consequences.

The tragedy in the Middle East started with a large-scale plot against international air traffic, carried out by the Palestine guerrillas who had been frustrated by the peace efforts. Within 72 hours four passenger aircraft belonging to American, British and Swiss companies were hijacked to the Middle East. A jumbo jet of Pan Am was blown up at Cairo Airport; six days later the same fate befell three jet planes, belonging to TWA, BOAC and Swissair, on the desert airstrip at Zerqa in Northern Jordan. The leaders of the Marxist "Popular Front for the Liberation of Palestine" had three objectives: the release of the Arab terrorists imprisoned in Western Europe, the punishment of the United States for supporting Israel, and the placing in the pillory of the régimes in Egypt and Jordan which were ready to negotiate.

The hijackings gave the final impetus to the outbreak of civil war in Jordan. King Hussein, in order to save his shaky throne, ordered his Bedouin troops to deal with the guerrilla problem. After the repulse of the Syrian intervention and a military victory achieved at a high cost in human suffering, the outcome of this "decisive struggle" was merely another agreement with the guerrillas. The day after the handshake between the opponents Hussein and Arafat, peacemaker Nasser died of a coronary attack. The "Rais" had transformed Egyptian nationalism into a pan-Arab one; for eighteen years he had sought a military solution of the Middle East problems, of which the Arabs in Israel were the incarnation; and only during the last weeks of his life had he adopted a conciliatory attitude. His sudden death undermined whatever stability remained after the worst crisis in the Middle East since the Six-Day War of 1967.

September 1 Unsuccessful attempt upon the life of King Hussein in Amman.

2 U.S. representations in Cairo and Moscow because of cease-fire violations.

3 Dr. Salvador Allende obtains largest share of the vote in Chile's Presidential election.

4 Three passenger aircraft hijacked to the Middle East by Palestine guerrillas.
Pan Am jumbo jet blown up in Cairo.

7 Privileges of Maharajas abolished in India.

8 Start of third summit conference of non-aligned nations in Lusaka.

9 BOAC plane hijacked to Zerqa desert airstrip. U.N. Security Council demands immediate release of hostages.

12 TWA, BOAC and Swissair hijacked planes blown up at Zerqa.

15 Cairo declares "Rogers" peace plan to be irrelevant.
King Hussein forms military government under Brigadier Mohammed Daoud and appoints Field-Marshal Habes Al-Majali as Commander-in-Chief and Military Governor.

17 Civil war breaks out in Jordan.

20 Syrian intervention in Northern Jordan.
Social Democrats lose absolute majority in Swedish general election but remain in power.

22 Tun Abdul Razak replaces Tunku Abdul Rahman as Prime Minister of Malaysia.

23 Syrian armoured units withdraw across frontier.

24 Automated spacecraft Luna 16 returns to earth with lunar rock.

25 Cease-fire in Jordanian civil war. Remaining hostages liberated by Hussein's troops.

27 Hussein and Arafat sign "final" peace agreement in Cairo.
President Nixon starts nine-day trip to Europe.

28 Egypt's President Gamal Abdel Nasser dies in Cairo, aged 52. Vice-President Anwar Sadat becomes Acting President.

30 Great Britain, the Federal Republic of Germany and Switzerland release the seven Arab hijackers held and deport them to Cairo.

4th September: Dr. *Salvador Allende*, physician and Senator, won the Presidential election in Chile. A loser in the 1952, 1958 and 1964 elections, Dr. Allende, a Marxist and leader of a coalition of the Left, narrowly defeated the independent conservative Jorge Alessandri. Radomiro Tomic, the candidate of the Christian Socialist Party of the outgoing President Eduardo Frei, came third. Allende's 36 per cent of the popular vote failed, however, to give him the necessary absolute majority. It therefore fell to Congress, according to the constitution, to choose the new President. The sensational victory of Allende, who is a friend of Fidel Castro, came as a shock to the upper classes in Chile. One result was a large-scale flow of capital out of the country even before the proclamation of the new President. (The pictures show Allende on horseback in a mountain village and as triumphant victor after the elections.)

5th September: After a number of fatal motor-racing accidents this year another world-famous driver was killed during a practice run for the 41st Italian Grand Prix at Monza. Following the death of New Zealand's Bruce McLaren and Britain's Piers Courage, the third Formula 1 driver to be killed was Austria's *Jochen Rindt*, aged 28, who held an overwhelming lead in the world championship. His Finnish wife, *Nina*, was as usual timing his laps from her stool among the British Lotus team, when the accident occurred during the fifth lap. Braking before the Parabolica corner, the Lotus 72 (No. 22) suddenly veered off the track, hit the guard rail and bounced back, breaking up in the process. Attempts to revive Rindt failed; he died of a ruptured trachea. But the world championship, for which Jochen Rindt had striven for so many years, remained his just the same. After five victories in eight races (Monaco, Zandvoort, Clermont-Ferrand, Brands Hatch and Hockenheim), his lead was invincible, neither Belgium's Jacky Ickx nor Switzerland's Clay Regazzoni could reach his points score during the remaining Grand Prix races. The tragedy at Monza again reopened the question as to whether there was any sense in continuing the hectic scramble to build ever faster and lighter racing cars. Jochen Rindt was the 37th first-class racing driver since the end of the war to pay with his life for his devotion to the sport. Twenty Grand Prix drivers have been killed on the tracks during the last ten years alone.

Rindt during his last race on the Monza circuit (top): in the fifth lap he came to grief.

The crashed car at the Parabolica corner: for Rindt it was the end.

Jochen Rindt, the posthumous world champion of the year 1970, was born in Mainz, but had grown up in Graz, where he was laid to rest.

6th September: Arab hijackers, with military precision, paralysed
international civil aviation with a whole series of outrages. Within a
period of 70 hours commandos of the "Popular Front for the
Liberation of Palestine" (PFLP) attacked five jets carrying a total of
650 passengers and 60 crew. Only one of these attacks failed, when
security guards and crew on board an El Al Boeing 707, which had
taken off from Amsterdam for New York, succeeded in thwarting the
hijackers. In the course of the fighting a terrorist from Nicaragua was
killed and a steward seriously injured. After the gunfight the plane
landed at Heathrow Airport, London. But the other four acts of
piracy were successful. A Boeing 747 jumbo jet of the "Pan American
World Airways" (Pan Am) with 150 passengers and a crew of 18 was
kidnapped between Amsterdam and New York and forced to stop at
Beirut, then fly to Cairo, where, a few minutes after landing it was
blown up. All that remained of the $20,000,000 giant jet was the
tailplane (above). Three other aircraft were forced to fly to Dawson's
Field (originally constructed by the British), near Zerqa in the desert
of Northern Jordan. For the past few weeks it had been in the hands
of the Fedayeen who had renamed it the "Airport of the Revolution".
The planes were a TWA Boeing 707 flying from Frankfurt to
New York, with 141 passengers and a crew of 10; a Swissair DC 8
bound from Zurich to New York, with 143 passengers and a crew
of 12; and a VC 10 belonging to BOAC, hijacked three days later
between Bahrein and Beirut, with 114 people aboard. The women,
children and sick passengers were taken to Amman in military buses,
while the remaining 310 passengers and crew were kept as hostages
on the desert airstrip, in almost unbearable conditions. The
"Popular Front" guerrillas blew up the three jet planes on
12th September (right). The aircraft were worth about £10 million.

A macabre press conference was held on the third day at the "Airport of the Revolution". Surrounded by armed guerrillas, some of the hostages were permitted to talk to journalists, with the aid of loudhailers, across a distance of 20 m. They complained about the heat and the terrible stench of the overflowing toilets in the aircraft.

After the three giant jets had been destroyed,
the almost unknown desert airstrip at Zerqa,
which had been the focus of world-wide
attention for a week, relapsed into obscurity.
Only the Bedouins were left to hunt for loot
among the torn fuselages and blackened
engines. Shortly before the planes were blown
up, the hostages were taken to Amman and all
but 55 released. The other passengers, who
had previously been taken to Jordan's capital,
had already been repatriated. On behalf of the
countries concerned—the United States,
Great Britain, Switzerland and West Germany,
who had formed a "crisis staff" in Berne and
were in close contact with Israel—the
International Committee of the Red Cross
(ICRC) sent a mission to Jordan to negotiate
with the "Popular Front for the Liberation of
Palestine" for the release of all the hostages.

In a 72-hour ultimatum, the PFLP threatened
to blow up the planes with the hostages inside,
unless the seven Arab terrorists held in Western
Europe were released. Among these was the most
notorious hijacker, 24-year-old *Leila Khaled* (right),
who had hijacked a TWA plane to Damascus and
blown it up there in August 1969, but failed in her
later attempt to gain control of an El Al airliner,
and was being held by the authorities in Britain.
The European governments being held to ransom
declared their readiness to meet the demands of the
guerrillas provided all hostages, including the Jews,
were released. The PFLP in return pressed for the
liberation of all guerrillas imprisoned in Israel.
This was refused by the Israeli Government. The
ICRC intervened to have the ultimatum extended
by 72 hours and finally lifted. Dr. *Georges Habash*
(below), the leader of the Popular Front, was in
North Korea at the time of the kidnappings. The
other guerrilla factions disassociated themselves from
the PFLP hijackings; even the extreme left-wing
"Democratic Popular Front for the Liberation of
Palestine", a splinter group of the PFLP, led by
Nayef Hawatmeh (below right), branded "these
gangster methods as lunacy which does nothing to
further the cause of revolution".

The hijackings to the "Airport of the Revolution" and the Fedayeen claim to Northern Jordan as "liberated territory" gave the final impetus to the long-expected test of strength between King Hussein and the Palestine guerrillas who formed a state within a state. Under pressure from his Army, which was unwilling to postpone a contest any longer, Hussein appointed Field-Marshal Habes Al-Majali of Bedouin origin, Commander-in-Chief and Military Governor. His task was to force the guerrilla organizations to remain quiet and observe law and order. When the Fedayeen declared war upon the new military régime and called the Jordanian population to armed revolt against the King, the conflict exploded into a bitter civil war. It was a battle of power, which had been fermenting since the Six-Day War of 1967, between the palace, with the support of the Army and the Bedouin tribes, and the Palestinian guerrillas. Violent fighting took place for the possession of the capital Amman, from which smoke could be seen rising skywards for many days (below). Strong armoured units from Syria advanced into Northern Jordan to support the guerrillas and threatened to transform the civil war in Jordan into an inter-Arab confrontation, or even an international conflict with unforeseen consequences. But the armoured columns, which had been given no air cover because of internal political squabbling, withdrew across the frontier after sustaining heavy losses. To the great disappointment of the Fedayeen the 12,000 Iraqi troops stationed in Jordan failed to intervene in the fighting despite the promises which had been made by Baghdad. The Palestinians, who felt betrayed, finally had to be thankful that mediation by the Arab countries saved them from total defeat.

After the withdrawal of the Syrian armoured units, which had moved to support the guerrillas in Northern Jordan (top right), the guerrilla organizations had virtually lost the contest. *Yassir Arafat*, their leader (centre right, with dark glasses), appealed unsuccessfully to the governments in Damascus and Baghdad, who had previously promised him support "to the last drop of blood", not to leave the Palestinians in the lurch. Not only did the civil war cause widespread destruction (the picture bottom right shows a devastated street in Amman), it also cost many lives. The Palestine Red Crescent reported 3,440 killed and 10,840 injured. Since all hospitals were overcrowded, badly injured children were flown to Beirut for treatment (top left).

President Nemery of the Sudan was sent by the Arab Heads of State, then meeting in Cairo, to Amman to mediate in the Jordanian civil war. After fierce fighting lasting for eight days, Nemery succeeded in persuading the contestants to call a halt to the fighting. In the presence of the Kings and Presidents gathered for the summit meeting in Cairo, King *Hussein* and the guerrilla leader *Yassir Arafat* then signed a "final agreement for the termination of the civil war". Egypt's President *Gamal Abdel Nasser*, watched the two rivals shake hands as a sign of their reconciliation (above). A committee under the leadership of Tunisia's Prime Minister Bahi Ladgham was formed to supervise the execution of the 14-point agreement which provided for the withdrawal of all armed forces from Amman. Although Hussein gained a fragile peace settlement, he lost his Prime Minister, Brigadier Mohammed Daoud, who requested political asylum from the Head of Libya's Revolutionary Council.

The role of peacemaker was to be the last political act of Egypt's President *Nasser*, shown on the right at Cairo airport welcoming King *Faisal* of Saudi Arabia on his arrival for the summit meeting.

The Sudanese Head of State, General *Jafaar al Nemery* (extreme right, with Kuwait's Minister of Defence As-Sabah) who acted as mediator, and succeeded in arranging an armistice in Amman at the second try.

The shock news of
Nasser's death caused
indescribable scenes of
grief and sorrow in Egypt.
Hundreds of thousands
openly sobbed in the
streets, calling "Nasser,
we are lost without you",
or "Nasser, you are not
dead. You will live till
victory. We all are
Nassers".

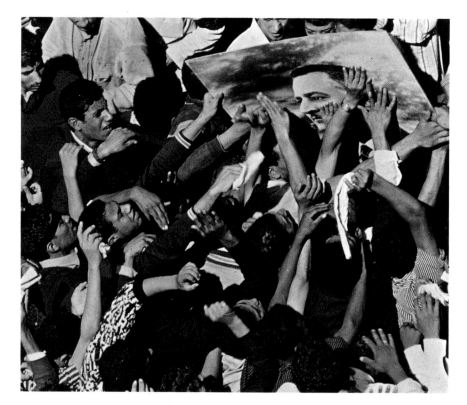

Eighteen Heads of State,
nine Prime Ministers and
delegations from over 70
countries accompanied
Nasser on his last journey
through Cairo. Millions
of grief-stricken Egyptians
thronged the 15-km route
of the funeral procession.

The day after Egypt's President *Gamal Abdel Nasser* had used his authority to
persuade Jordan's King Hussein and Palestinian leader Yassir Arafat to make
peace, he died in Cairo following an attack of coronary thrombosis, aged 52.
The death of this charismatic statesman, who had been the central figure in
Middle East politics for almost two decades and had given the Arabs back their
self-confidence, caused consternation and violent grief in the whole Arab world.
He was the idol of his people, despite the fact that all his ambitious plans had
failed. The death of the only man strong enough to lead the Arab world to peace,
once more called into question the hopes for a settlement of the troubles in the
Middle East, which had been revived after the cease-fire along the Suez Canal.

Bereft of their senses, the milling crowds
at the funeral procession pressed
towards the coffin, which had to be
defended with rifle butts and truncheons
by officers and soldiers fighting their
last battle for Nasser. Millions of hands
seemed to be determined to keep him
from his grave. Such an outbreak of mass
hysteria had never been witnessed
before. Five thousand army cadets had
to fight their way through the crowds to
protect the cortege of "the last Pharoah".
When the modest wooden coffin reached
its destination, it had to be lowered
into the tomb without a flag.

After the hijackings to the Middle East, the international airlines introduced stricter security measures to deal with aerial piracy. The search of passengers and luggage by magnetic screens and other electronic equipment was employed by airport police to find hidden guns, grenades and plastic bombs. The controls at the airports from which the flights of the recently hijacked aircraft had started were particularly strict. The Swiss Government decided to protect the airports at Zurich-Kloten and Geneva-Cointrin by deploying soldiers armed with automatic weapons and live ammunition (above). Hitherto only the Israeli airline El Al had used armed security guards aboard its planes. Now Swissair also decided to adopt this controversial measure.

Stricter controls on the ground
were introduced to thwart
abduction in the air: electronic
detectors at London's Heathrow
Airport (above) and searching of
passengers at Amsterdam's
Schiphol Airport (left).

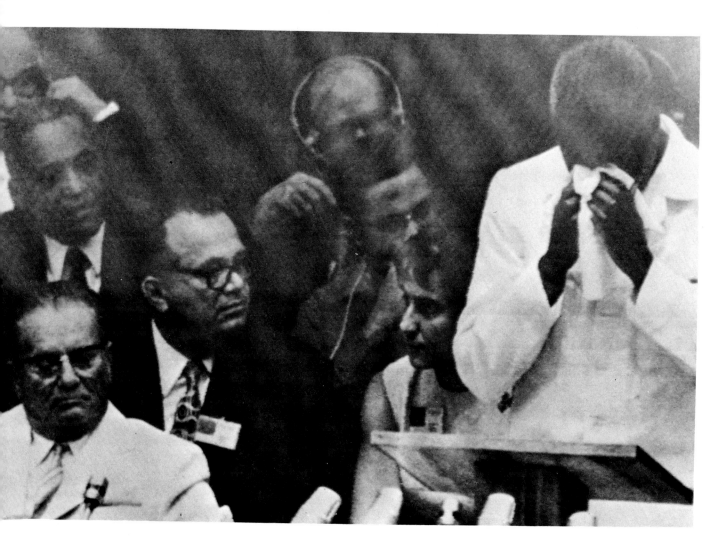

8th September: As *Kenneth Kaunda*, Zambia's President, was opening the summit conference of non-aligned nations in Lusaka, and deploring the fate of his black brothers suppressed by white minority governments, he suddenly buried his face in his hands and burst into sobs. For 5 minutes there was an embarrassed silence at the meeting attended by 54 non-aligned nations. Three days later the 17 Heads of State, eight Prime Ministers and 29 other Heads of Delegations approved a declaration which stated: "The immediate danger of a conflict between the superpowers has lessened since, in their own interest, they are inclined to negotiate. This does not, however, represent a contribution to the security of the small and medium-sized nations and of the developing countries, nor does it exclude the possibility of a local war. The balance of terror between the superpowers has brought neither peace nor security to the rest of the world." But the Lusaka conference, presided over by Yugoslavia's President *Tito* (bottom left of picture), had made it clear that the "Third World" could not make a decisive impact upon international politics while it had internal differences.

20th September: Serious incidents occurred in front of the congress building in Copenhagen during the opening of the annual meeting of the World Bank and the International Monetary Fund. Thousands of young Danish and Swedish students protested against the World Bank and its President, Robert McNamara, the former U.S. Secretary for Defence, and threw Molotov cocktails at the police. Inside the building the conference delegates from 116 countries were mainly concerned with measures to fight inflation. Bonn's Economics Minister Schiller called inflation a drug "which briefly makes our society high. But after the trip follows the inevitable rude awakening."

18th September: Jimi Hendrix, the 27-year-old guitarist and singer, one of the most famous stars of pop music, died in London. Part Negro and part Indian, this pop singer from Seattle, U.S.A., smashed his instruments during concerts and drove hundreds of thousands to ecstasy by his virtuosity.

20th September: The first Swedish general election after the parliamentary reform (introducing a 350-seat single chamber parliament instead of the previous bicameral system) failed to produce the shift in power forecast by the opinion pollsters. But the Social Democrats with 162 seats, led by 43-year-old Prime Minister *Olaf Palme*, lost their absolute majority for the first time to the conservative opposition parties, who won a total of 171 seats. However, Palme (shown above left looking for the key to his terraced house in Stockholm after a strenuous election night) rejected the offer to form a coalition with *Gunnar Hedlund* (above right), the 70-year-old leader of the Centre Party, because he was able to rely upon the support of the 17 Communists elected to parliament. The Communists saw themselves obliged to support sole government by the Social Democrats in order to avoid the fall of Palme and a take-over of power by a right-wing coalition.

20th September: Three months after snatching the traditionally Gaullist town of Nancy from the Gaullists in a by-election, *Jean-Jacques Servan-Schreiber* made his second challenge. This time he stood as a candidate in the Bordeaux by-election against Prime Minister *Jacques Chaban-Delmas.* But he miscalculated his chances against the local celebrity and Mayor of Bordeaux for the past 23 years. After an election campaign conducted in the American style, Servan-Schreiber (above, talking to the owner of a shoe shop) obtained a mere 16·59 per cent of the votes, while Chaban-Delmas won 63·55 per cent, more than ever before. This strengthened the unshakable position of Chaban-Delmas within his own party (left, he is seen talking to a newspaper seller).

21st September: The first attempt to cross the Atlantic by balloon was started from East Hampton on Long Island (New York State). 32-year-old British flight engineer *Malcom Brighton* (right, in the basket), U.S. stockbroker *Rodney Anderson* of the same age (left), and the latter's wife *Pamela*, aged 28, hoped to make the journey in a combined gas/hot air balloon christened "Free Life". The only member of the crew with any experience was Brighton, who predicted that their 5600-km journey to Paris would take four to six days. But the inadequately prepared project ended in disaster. As early as the second day the balloon was struck by a gale and they reported that their altitude had dropped from 1000 to 185 m and they were getting ready to splash down into the sea. That was the last message from "Free Life". U.S. Coast Guard vessels and aircraft searched in vain for several days in the Cape Race area off St John's, Newfoundland, but failed to find any trace of the ballon or its occupants.

24th September: The Soviet Union succeeded in carrying out the first soft landing of an unmanned spacecraft on the moon and bringing it back to earth. Luna 16, with the help of a drilling device controlled from the earth, obtained lunar rock samples from depths of up to 35 cm in the Sea of Fertility. These samples were transferred into a hermetically sealed container which, suspended from a parachute, landed in the steppes of the Central Asian Soviet Republic (right), after it had detached itself from the spacecraft when it was approaching the earth.

25th September: The death occurred of the famous writer *Erich Maria Remarque*, aged 72, in a hospital at Locarno. His anti-war classic "All Quiet on the Western Front" written in 1927 and translated into 45 languages with more than eight million copies printed, made him one of the most widely read authors of the century. During the Second World War, when he was in exile, he became a U.S. citizen, but after the war he returned to his house on the shore of Lake Maggiore. "Arc de Triomphe", his refugee novel published in 1946, also achieved world-wide success. His third marriage was to the film-star Paulette Goddard.

27th September: The nine-day European trip of
U.S. President *Richard Nixon*, which was intended
to underline the American presence in the
Mediterranean, was overshadowed by the sudden
death of Egypt's President Nasser. The news of
Nasser's death reached the President aboard the
aircraft carrier "Saratoga" (above right), where he
was attending the manoeuvres of the Mediterranean
based U.S. Sixth Fleet. Earlier Nixon had visited
Italy, a NATO partner, where he and his wife *Pat*
were received at the Quirinale Palace in Rome by
President *Giuseppe Saragat* and Prime Minister
Emilio Colombo, in office for the past two months
(above). The third stop of the trip (centre right) was
Belgrade, where Marshal *Tito* welcomed the first
American President to visit Yugoslavia, with
restrained friendship. Subsequently, contrary to the
planned programme, Tito accompanied Nixon to his
native village of Kumrovec, where the two
Presidents exchanged childhood memories seated on
a bed in the house in which Tito was born. In
Madrid their reception formed a noticeable contrast
to the anti-American demonstrations in Italy and
the studied restraint in Yugoslavia. Nixon was
warmly welcomed by Spain's President
Generalissimo *Francisco Franco* at the airport
(bottom picture) and cheered by more than a
million people during his drive along the avenues of
the Spanish capital. Nixon, who had been accused
by his political opponents at home of having
planned his trip with the coming mid-term elections
in mind, stated enthusiastically that it had been the
largest crowd ever assembled for an occasion of
this kind.

During his five-hour stop-over in Great Britain, President *Nixon* and
Prime Minister *Edward Heath* discussed the Middle East situation and
East-West relations. A lunch given by the Prime Minister in honour of
his guest and Mrs Nixon, at the country residence of Chequers, was also
attended by Queen *Elizabeth II*, who had interrupted her holiday in
Scotland. It was the first time that the Queen had been a guest and not
hostess on such an occasion. The last three days of Nixon's trip were
spent in Ireland (above on his way from Shannon to Limerick), where
the President met his Chief Negotiator at the Paris Vietnam talks,
David Bruce, to discuss a new peace initiative for Indo-China.

65-year-old *Karl Wallenda*, leader of one of the most famous teams of tightrope walkers in the world, crowned his career as an artiste by performing the boldest feat of his life. He crossed the gorge of the Tallulah waterfalls in Georgia, U.S.A., on a 330-m long wire suspended 210 m above the ground. Twice he knelt down, placed the balancing pole on the wire and performed a faultless handstand, frightening the life out of the 35,000 spectators.

October

Anwar Sadat takes over as Nasser's successor: Egypt's new President offering prayers in the mosque of his native village.

The terror of kidnapping strikes again, this time in Canada: Pierre Laporte, Minister of Labour, is abducted and murdered (shown here a few days before his kidnapping in conversation with reporters).

The kidnapping of public figures as a means of political blackmail moved outside the arena of Latin America and into a country with a democratic constitution based on the rule of law. In Canada the British Trade Commissioner to Montreal, James Cross, and the Canadian Minister of Labour and Immigration, Pierre Laporte, were abducted by members of the "Front for the Liberation of Quebec" (FLQ) organization. The French-Canadian separatists demanded the release of 23 "political" prisoners (condemned for murder, manslaughter, arson, bank robberies and bomb attacks) in return for Pierre Laporte. The dilemma facing the Liberal Prime Minister Pierre Trudeau and his Government was either to give way and so encourage the repetition of terrorist acts, or to risk the lives of the hostages. Their refusal to submit to this extortionist blackmail resulted in the cowardly murdering of Pierre Laporte by his captors.

In contrast to Canada, where a small group of left-wing extremists wanted to force their will upon the large majority of the people, democracy in Chile had to undergo its baptism of fire against a conspiracy by right-wing extremists, who tried to prevent the assumption of power by the Marxist President Salvador Allende. They attempted to involve the army in politics, against the traditions of the country, by attacking the Commander-in-Chief, René Schneider. But the democratic elements, headed by the outgoing President Eduardo Frei, succeeded in defeating the plot and carried through the installation of Chile's new President. Allende had previously assured his political opponents that he would maintain the democratic system.

The choice of Nasser's successor in Egypt was resolved with unexpected speed thus preventing internal strife between contestants for his position. The new President, Anwar Sadat, who had been Nasser's faithful supporter for 32 years and like his predecessor belonged to the conspiratorial group of the "Free Officers", did not want to perpetuate Nasser's authoritarian style of rule: he turned to the principle of collective leadership.

October 2 President Nixon visits Spain.
3 President Nixon visits Great Britain and Eire.
5 Acting President Sadat nominated candidate in the Egyptian Presidential election.
James Cross, British Trade Commissioner in Montreal, kidnapped by members of the FLQ.
6 Power struggle in Bolivia: General Miranda, after the enforced resignation of President Ovando, proclaims himself President, but is pushed aside by General Torres, a left-wing nationalist, who is nominated President.
Arthur and Nizamodeen Hosein jailed for life after 16-day trial at Old Bailey for kidnapping and murder of Mrs. Muriel McKay (wife of newspaper director).
7 Egypt's National Assembly elects Sadat as President.
8 1970 Nobel Prize for Literature awarded to Soviet writer Alexander Solzhenitsyn.
9 Cambodia proclaimed a republic.
10 Canadian Minister Pierre Laporte kidnapped by FLQ.
Fiji granted independence after 96 years of British rule.
11 President Tito visits President Brandt.
13 Canada recognizes Chinese People's Republic.
14 North Vietnam officially rejects President Nixon's peace plan.
15 Egyptian people endorse Sadat as President.
Iraq's Vice-President Hardan Takriti dismissed.

1970 Nobel Prize for Medicine awarded to Ulf von Euler (Sweden), Sir Bernard Katz (Britain) and Julius Axelrod (United States).
Two Lithuanians hijack Aeroflot plane to Turkey; pilot injured, stewardess killed.
16 President Trudeau invokes state of emergency in Canada.
18 Laporte's body found at the outskirts of Montreal.
Syrian Prime Minister Dr. Noureddin Atassi resigns.
20 Former Foreign Minister Mahmoud Fawzi becomes Egypt's Prime Minister.
Exiled Algerian politician Belkacem Krim found murdered at Frankfurt hotel.
Half a million reported homeless and 750 dead after typhoon hits Philippines.
21 1970 Nobel Prize for Peace awarded to Norman Ernest Borlaug (United States).
Soviet Union holds two U.S. generals after their plane is forced down in Armenia.
24 Salvador Allende proclaimed President of Chile by Congress.
26 Nobel Prize for Economics awarded to Paul A. Samuelson (United States).
27 Nobel Prize for Physics awarded to Hannes Alfven (Sweden) and Louis Néel (France).
Nobel Prize for Chemistry awarded to Luis Leloir (Argentina).
Soviet students hijack Aeroflot plane to Turkey.
28 Wasfi Tall succeeds Ahmed Toukan as Prime Minister of Jordan.
30 Gromyko visits Federal Republic of Germany.

1st October: Riots in five New York prisons resulted in the capture of 26 hostages by the prisoners, who demanded improved conditions, including better sanitary facilities, a speeding up of court procedures, and fairer treatment by the warders. They also protested against the overcrowding of the cells. One prison built to hold 194 inmates (the picture on the left shows protesting prisoners at a cell window), held 338 prisoners at the time of the riot. Amongst these were prisoners on remand who, despite minor offences, had been in custody for as long as six months. At Long Island Prison prisoners (some of whom wore picturesque attire) were given the opportunity of participating in a hearing in the prison courtyard in order to present their complaints to officials and elected representatives (below right *Shirley Chisholm*, Democratic Congresswoman). After Mayor Lindsay had accepted that the complaints were justified and promised action, the hostages were set free.

A sign of life from the kidnapped British diplomat: a picture received which shows *James Cross* in captivity. On the reverse, signed in his handwriting, there is the following message from his kidnappers: "Despite everything, the smiling Mr. Cross feels reassured after being told that Bourassa cannot be as inhuman as he is made out to be".

M CROSS, SOURIANT
EST QUAND MÊME
RÊCONFORTÉ
LORSQU'ON·LUI
DIT QUE
BOURASSA NE PEUT
PAS ETRE AUSSI INHUMAIN
QU'IL LE LAISSE VOIR

5th October: Following the example of Latin American guerrillas, a commando of the "Front for the Liberation of Quebec" (FLQ) kidnapped 49-year-old *James Richard Cross*, the British Trade Commissioner in Montreal. The kidnappers threatened to execute him unless the Canadian Government released 23 members of the FLQ under arrest and flew them to Cuba or Algeria, paid a ransom of $500,000 in gold, broadcast a FLQ manifesto and surrendered an informer who had betrayed an FLQ cell to the police. The Government in Ottawa rejected these demands and merely offered the kidnappers free exit from the country in return for the kidnapped diplomat. This provoked the militant French-Canadian separatist movement, which had become notorious through its numerous bomb outrages during the last seven years, to strike again. Armed masked men kidnapped 49-year-old Pierre Laporte, Minister of Labour and Immigration for the Province of Quebec. Even after this coup, however, the Canadian Government refused to give way. In agreement with Robert Bourassa, Prime Minister of the Quebec Provincial Government, Canada's Prime Minister Trudeau invoked for the first time in peacetime the War Measures Act, sent troops into the Province of Quebec to support the police and outlawed the FLQ. Immediately after the declaration of the state of emergency, police and troops carried out a massive search for the kidnappers and their victims in Montreal and made mass arrests throughout Quebec Province. Among those arrested was Robert Lemieux, the lawyer who had been negotiating with the authorities on behalf of the FLQ about the release of Cross and Laporte.

Pierre Laporte, the kidnapped Minister, was a journalist before joining the Quebec Provincial Government. He was the head of a large family. In addition to his own two children, he acted as guardian to the children of two brothers who had died.

The FLQ reacted to the moves of the Canadian Government by murdering the kidnapped Labour Minister Pierre Laporte after he had sent a desperate appeal for help. After the arrest of his kidnappers it was learnt that he had made an abortive attempt to escape on the eve of his execution. Laporte's body was found in the boot of the car used by the FLQ terrorists when they kidnapped him: the Chevrolet was parked near an airfield 5 kilometres east of Montreal. Laporte had been strangled and his corpse showed signs of torture. The Prime Minister *Pierre Elliott Trudeau* (below) was visibly shaken and declared that, as a Canadian, he felt ashamed that such a "cruel and senseless act" had been perpetrated. The most extensive security measures in Canada's history were taken for the funeral in Montreal Cathedral, which was attended by Trudeau, several of his Ministers and numerous members of parliament. Before the funeral the police discovered the house in the suburb of St. Hubert in which Laporte had been held as a captive and murdered. The bungalow had been rented by a teacher Paul Rose, a member of the Chenier cell of the FLQ, which had organized Laporte's kidnapping. The few hundred activists of the FLQ are organized in cells comprising three to five men, each cell operating independently, with the aim of creating a new Vietnam in Canada.

After the imposition of the state of emergency Montreal resembled an armed camp. The picture left shows troops surrounding a block suspected of containing the hideout of the kidnappers of Mr. Cross.

Juliette Laporte, the mother of the murdered Minister, almost collapsed after identifying the body of her son.

The wooden bungalow in the suburb of St. Hubert, scene of Laporte's captivity and murder. It was in this deserted bungalow that police found the shirt worn by the Minister at the time of his kidnapping.

6th October: Bolivia, a country which has experienced no fewer than 184 coups d'état during her 145-year history, set up a new record by changing its government four times in the space of two days. The game of musical chairs started with the overthrow of 57-year-old President *Alfredo Ovando Candia*. He had seized power in September 1969 and had initiated a "national revolution" with a trend towards the left, following the example of the progressive generals in neighbouring Peru. This had been unexpected since he had previously been responsible for the death of "Che" Guevara when Commander-in-Chief of the Bolivian armed forces. Right-wing officers, who disapproved of the President's zigzag policy, therefore rose against Ovando during his absence from the capital. His supporters nevertheless carried him into the Presidential Palace on his return (above left), but he resigned in order to avoid civil war. The arch-conservative Head of the Army, 46-year-old General *Rogelio Miranda* (above right), then proclaimed himself the new President. His intention was to impose extreme right-wing policies upon the country. However, after encountering strong resistance, he installed a three-man military junta consisting of General Efrain Guachalla, Chief of the General Staff of the Armed Forces; General Fernando Sattori, Chief of the Air Force; and Rear-Admiral Alberto Albarracin, in charge of the Navy. In the meantime, the former Commander-in-Chief of the Armed Forces, General *Juan José Torres*, proclaimed himself "Revolutionary President of Bolivia". Torres, a 49-year-old left-wing nationalist, who had been relieved of his functions by Ovando in July, was now carried into power by a spontaneous alliance of young officers, armed peasants, workers and students. Even the members of the junta eventually gave him their support. Miranda had to seek refuge in the Paraguayan Embassy. At the end of the two-day struggle for power, the left-wing Bolivian general entered the Presidential Palace of La Paz. After his inauguration President Torres, from the balcony of the palace (right), promised the crowd clamouring for a "people's government" that his administration would be based on four pillars: the peasants, the workers, the students and the armed forces.

6th October: Hundreds of onlookers who gathered in front of the registry office at Caxton Hall in London, did not come to see the newly married couple, but the bridegroom's beautiful mother, film-star *Elizabeth Taylor* (left). The 18-year-old bridegroom *Michael Wilding*, who was clad in a chestnut-coloured velvet caftan and wearing sandals, offered a far from ordinary spectacle. The 19-year-old bride *Beth Clutter*, daughter of an American oceanologist, wore a simple white satin dress. She is seen (below) with *Richard Burton*, Elizabeth Taylor's husband and her 13-year-old daughter *Liza Todd*. The bridegroom's father, the British actor Michael Wilding, was Elizabeth Taylor's second husband.

Princess *Zahra*, the first child of 33-year-old *Karim Aga Khan IV* and 30-year-old Begum *Salima* (previously Lady Crichton-Stuart), was "officially" photographed with her parents for the first time since her birth on the 18th September. The 15 million adherents of the Muslim Ismaili sect, mainly to be found in East Africa and the Middle East, were disappointed that their spiritual leader had not become the father of a healthy son and heir. However, the Aga Khan let it be known that he was by no means disappointed that the Begum had "only" presented him with a girl.

6th October: Two months after the conclusion of the Russo-German treaty the French President, *Georges Pompidou*, visited the Soviet Union. The outcome was an agreement with the Moscow leaders for regular consultations to take place twice yearly, or more frequently when necessary, between the Foreign Ministers of France and the Soviet Union. In the picture above Pompidou is seen in the Kremlin with Party Leader *Leonid Brezhnev*, President *Nikolai Podgorny* and Prime Minister *Alexei Kosygin*. As a gesture of friendship Pompidou promised French support for the all-European security conference, which Brezhnev had been planning for a long time. While the President of France was busy talking politics with the Soviet leaders, the elegant Madame *Claude Pompidou* (second from the left) discussed women's problems with *Elena Alekseyevna Podgornaya*, who is rarely seen in public (left), *Viktoria Brezhneva* (second from the right), and the wife of the First Deputy Prime Minister Dmitriy Polyansky. During their eight-day state visit the French visitors inspected the space centre at Baikonur and the cities of Novosibirsk, Tashkent and Samarkand.

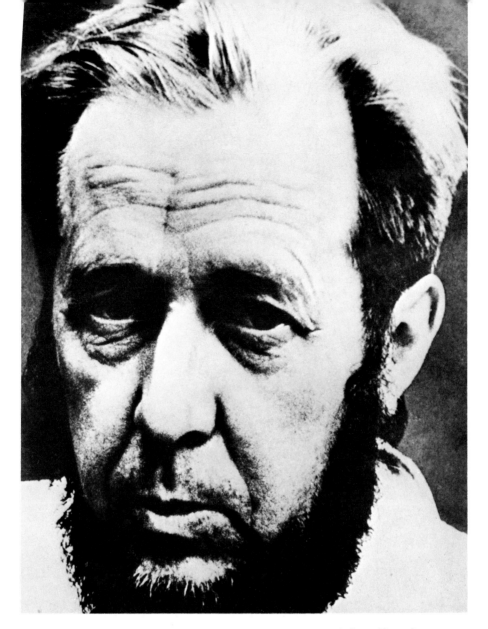

8th October: The 1970 Nobel Prize for Literature was awarded to *Alexander Solzhenitsyn*, the Russian writer who in his own country is branded an "enemy" and "traitor". The Swedish Academy justified its decision to bestow the most distinguished literary award in the world upon the 51-year-old author of the novels "Cancer Ward" and "First Circle", on the grounds of the ethical force with which he has pursued the indispensable traditions of Russian literature. In contrast to Boris Pasternak, who was awarded the prize in 1958 and also persecuted by the régime, Solzhenitsyn accepted the prize and expressed the wish to personally attend the award ceremony in Stockholm. However, he was later forced to cancel his proposed journey because of the risk that he would be barred from returning to Russia. Solzhenitsyn was a Captain in charge of an anti-aircraft battery near Leningrad during the Second World War, but was imprisoned without trial in 1945 and spent eight years in Stalin's prisons and labour camps. In the period of the cultural thaw under Khrushchev, Solzhenitsyn was rehabilitated for a brief period but in recent times he has been persecuted by the régime and was expelled from the Writers' Union in 1969. The poet Yevtushenko has described him as "our only living classic".

9th October: With due pomp and ceremony Cambodia was proclaimed a republic in Phnom Penh, the capital. This step, which signified the end of the 1,900-year-old Khmer monarchy, had been announced several times since the overthrow of Prince Norodom Sihanouk, the Head of State, on 18th March, 1970. Sihanouk was the last but one of the Khmer kings: he ascended to the throne in 1941, but abdicated in 1955 in favour of his father in order to take a more active role in politics. After his father's death in 1960 a new king was not elected (Cambodia was an elective monarchy), although the Prince's mother was recognized as the symbol of the monarchy. While the exiled Sihanouk in Peking protested against the proclamation of the republic and appealed for aid to the monarchies of Great Britain, Japan, Thailand and Laos, General *Lon Nol*, the Prime Minister, hailed the event as the "finest day of our history". The picture shows Lon Nol being congratulated by Buddhist monks on the occasion of the constitutional change.

10th October: On the 59th anniversary of the foundation of the Chinese Republic, 84-year-old Generalissimo *Chiang Kai-shek*, the President of Nationalist China, once again promised the return of the Nationalists to mainland China. From in front of the Presidential Palace in Taipeh, his provisional capital on Formosa, Chiang Kai-shek, who had been driven out of China by the Communists in 1949, told his 250,000 listeners that the decisive battle against "Mao and his band" was inevitable for the restoration of peace to the Chinese people after decades of civil war. He said that 70 per cent of the fight for national revolution was being waged by political means and 30 per cent by military means; the re-conquest of the mainland was only a question of time.

13th October: Canada's recognition of the Chinese People's Republic dealt a heavy blow to the disintegrating anti-Peking front in the United Nations. During the twenty months of negotiations the Communist Chinese claim to the island of Formosa had been the main obstacle to the resumption of diplomatic relations between Ottawa and Peking. Canada refused to formally recognize this claim and in the end merely "noted" it. In Formosa, the Nationalist Chinese Government reacted to this decision by Canada, which was followed by Italy a few weeks later, by immediately breaking off diplomatic relations and recalling *Yu-chi Hsueh*, its Ambassador, who is shown in the picture above taking leave from his compatriots before leaving Ottawa.

14th October: After a hunt lasting nine weeks *Angela Davis* (right), a 26-year-old civil rights militant, was arrested in a New York motel. This lecturer in sociology and philosophy at the University of California, who was once Herbert Marcuse's favourite disciple, had been placed on the FBI's list of most wanted fugitives. She was charged with being an accessory to murder and kidnapping, and accused of having supplied arms for the attempted escape by prisoners from the courthouse at San Rafael (California) on 7th August. The judge, an accomplice and two prisoners had lost their lives during the attempt. In order to disguise her appearance, the "Jeanne d'Arc of the Black Panthers" had hidden her African-style hair under a wig of short hair and replaced her original spectacles by a set of fashionable horn-rimmed ones. In the weeks that followed her arrest the coloured lecturer, because of her Communist beliefs, fought in vain to avoid extradition to California.

15th October: In Egypt, while a group of stonemasons were working on Nasser's tombstone (top right), a national referendum was held to decide upon a successor to the deceased Head of State. Acting President *Anwar Sadat*, nominated by the Central Committee of the Arab Socialist Union and unanimously endorsed by the National Assembly, won 90·04 per cent of the votes cast, and was duly elected President for the next six years. 52-year-old Sadat (second from the right in the picture above, at the laying of the foundation stone of the Nasser Memorial Research Institute in Cairo) declared that neither he nor anybody else had the force to assume Nasser's burden. This made a new distribution of responsibilities necessary. The former Foreign Minister, Mahmoud Fawzi, was appointed Prime Minister and the former Deputy Prime Minister, Abdel Mohsen Abu el Nur, Secretary-General of the official party. However, Sadat succeeded in achieving within weeks something that had eluded his predecessor all his life: he persuaded the Heads of States of Libya and of the Sudan, Colonel *Moamer al Kadhafi* (right) and General *Jaafar al Nemery* (third from right), of the need for a union between their three Arab states.

The controversial maxi fashion which, against the determined opposition of all male and female mini fans, had gradually made headway during the year, succeeded in consolidating and extending its position during the cold season. The Après ski collection presented by the Paris fashion designer Paco Rabanne, famous for his dresses made of metal and plastics, was dominated by the maxi. It was evident that women wearing his luminous dresses would command undivided attention even in the most exclusive winter sports resorts.

20th October: 48-year-old *Belkacem Krim*, the exiled Algerian politician, was found strangled at the Intercontinental Hotel in Frankfurt. He had been one of the moving spirits in the Algerian revolution and was responsible for negotiating the independence of his country at the Evian Conference in 1962. He subsequently fell out with Ben Bella and has since been living in exile in Lausanne. The Algerian revolutionary and leader of the Kabyles was sentenced to death by the French on several occasions during the war of liberation. In 1969 he was again sentenced to death in his absence by an Algerian military tribunal at Oran. Was his death the execution of the sentence ? Belkacem Krim was thought to have been the instigator of the military revolt of December 1967, and of the attacks against the Minister of Finance Ahmed and the President Boumedienne.

22nd October: General *René Schneider*, Commander-in-Chief of Chile's Army, was fatally wounded by eight shots while travelling by his car to the Ministry of Defence in Santiago. The attack, which was carried out by right-wing extremists, was intended to provoke an Army revolt and thereby prevent the Marxist Dr. Salvador Allende being nominated President by Congress. The 56-year-old General, who had promised to respect the "decision of the ballot boxes", was an obstacle to the plans of the extremists. "His respect for the constitution cost him his life", said the new President, when Schneider succumbed to his injuries the day after Congress had confirmed Allende's appointment as President.

24th October: The collision between the two oil tankers "Allegro" (46,402 tons) and "Pacific Glory" (42,777 tons) in the English Channel caused the death of thirteen Chinese seamen. Both ships were sailing under the Liberian flag. The accident threatened the English coast with pollution on the same scale as that which occurred after the "Torrey Canyon" disaster off the Scilly Islands in 1967. The badly damaged "Pacific Glory", with 70,000 tons of crude oil on board, later caught fire after several explosions in the engine room. It took 40 hours to bring the blaze under control. The helpless drifting wreck was taken in tow by sea-going tugs and grounded off the Isle of Wight. In a desperate race against time British salvage experts succeeded in preventing the vessel from breaking up and thereby avoided a large-scale disaster.

24th October: The celebrations to mark the 25th anniversary of the founding of the United Nations were overshadowed by discord between the member countries. In contrast to U Thant, the U.N. Secretary-General, who was prepared "despite everything" to produce a positive balance-sheet, many of the speakers stressed the disappointments rather than the achievements of the world organization. In addition, President *Richard Nixon* created competition for the official anniversary celebration by holding a state banquet: many Heads of State and Prime Ministers preferred dinner in the White House to the birthday cake in the U.N. building. Seated on the far side of the table are President *François Tombalbaye* of Chad, Mrs. *Pat Nixon,* the hostess, Emperor *Haile Selassie* of Ethiopia, the U.S. President, and President *Urho Kekkonen* of Finland. The latter, in his speech to the General Assembly of the United Nations, reproachfully stated that during the past 25 years the problems of the world had been "talked into shreds" at the U.N. However, it is worth noting that since its foundation in San Francisco, the membership of the U.N. has grown from 50 to 127 nations.

It was not only in London's Berkeley Square, where according to a popular song "the nightingale sang", that a stench rose to high heaven. There were mountains of rotting garbage on the squares and streets of many British towns after council workers went on strike at the beginning of the month in support of a 55/- wage claim. The Government refused to negotiate for fear that its incomes policy would be swamped by inflationary wage demands. The situation was made worse by the fact that it was not only the refuse collectors who had stopped work, but also the drainage workers, road sweepers and sewage workers. It took five weeks before the parties involved in the dispute, under considerable pressure from public opinion, reached a settlement.

November

France mourns a great man: the grave of General Charles de Gaulle in the village churchyard of Colombey-les-Deux-Eglises, surrounded by wreaths and flowers.

Disease and hunger followed the worst flood disaster of the century: a woman begging for food in East Pakistan's disaster area.

The last of the grand old men of Europe, Charles de Gaulle, died on the evening of 9th November, in the peace and quiet of "La Boisserie", his country home in Lorraine. It was not the first time that he had been confronted by death: in 1916, when as a Captain in the French Army he made a heroic assault at Verdun and was so badly wounded he was believed to be dead; in 1944, when he was shot at by a German sniper as he entered Notre Dame to hear Mass for the liberation of Paris; and more recently in 1962, when he was machine-gunned by OAS terrorists at Petit-Clamart. Charles de Gaulle died as he had lived, bravely and with dignity. His simple funeral in the rural setting of Colombey-les-Deux-Eglises, organized in accordance with his instructions in his will, contained that same quality of dignity. One of the outstanding figures of his time, the only question that remains to be answered by history is whether his achievements will prove greater than his errors.

Never before had an American President played such a prominent part in the mid-term elections as Richard Nixon. He rushed from one election meeting to the next, covering 22 States and preaching the politics of polarization which Vice-President Spiro T. Agnew had previously expounded in 29 States. Both of them restricted their campaign to a single theme, that of "law and order", eschewing any alternative solutions for the problems of a society in turmoil. By stirring up latent fears in a manner reminiscent of Macchiavelli they managed to sow discord even within their own ranks. The "silent majority", which Nixon and Agnew had quoted so frequently in the past remained silent. Was it the silent majority in California that chose a liberal Democrat to represent the State as Senator in Washington, but simultaneously retained a conservative Republican in office as Governor? If it really existed, it left the President in the lurch during his assault on the Capitol, for the Democrats remained in control of both Houses of Congress. Nixon was forced to continue as President with Congress against him. Coupled with an ailing economy and a growing number of unemployed this gave him little ground for optimism when looking ahead to gauge his prospects of being re-elected in 1972.

November 1 Polish Deputy Foreign Minister Zygfryd Wolniak killed in attack on Polish delegation in Karachi.
Dance-hall fire at St-Laurent-du-Pont (France) kills 145.

3 U.S. mid-term elections: Democratic gains in House of Representatives, minor losses in Senate.

6 Three months' Suez cease-fire extended.
Italy enters into diplomatic relations with Chinese People's Republic.

9 Death of General de Gaulle at Colombey-les-Deux-Eglises.

10 EEC starts exploratory talks with Switzerland, Sweden and Austria.

12 De Gaulle buried at Colombey-les-Deux-Eglises. Official Requiem Mass at Notre Dame Cathedral in Paris.

13 Hundreds of thousands of victims in East Pakistan flood disaster.
Military coup in Syria: General Hafez Assad assumes power.

16 Luna 17 lands remote-control moon crawler, Lunokhod 1 on the moon.

18 Ahmad Khatib becomes Syria's new President.

21 U.S. airborne assault fails to liberate prisoners near Hanoi.

22 Guinea asks U.N. for help to repel invasion by mercenaries.

25 Nobel Prize candidate Yukio Mishima commits hara-kiri in Yokyo.

26 Pope Paul VI embarks upon his longest foreign trip to Asia and Australia.

27 Pope Paul VI narrowly escapes assassination in Manila.

1st November: All Saints' Day became a national day of
mourning for France: 145 young people lost their lives
when the "5-7" dance hall at St-Laurent-du-Pont,
near Grenoble, caught fire and was burnt to the ground.
The occasion was a Saturday night dance attended by a
large number of young people from a wide area. It turned
into a dance of death, after a carelessly discarded
cigarette end set fire to the plastic decorations and
furniture. The blaze spread rapidly and because the
proprietors had locked the four emergency exits to thwart
gate-crashers, the main exit, which was through turnstiles
became blocked and turned into a death trap.
Only forty people escaped from the inferno, eleven of
them badly burned. The dance hall had no telephone,
so that the fire brigade arrived too late and the hydrant in
front of the building was found unconnected. President
Pompidou immediately ordered an enquiry into the
catastrophe. The Mayor of St-Laurent-du-Pont and the
General Secretary of the Isère Department were suspended
for having authorized the opening of the establishment
and twice extended its licence, although the dance hall
had not been vetted by the fire services.

The most expensive section of the Swiss motorway network, on the shores of the Lake of Geneva, was opened to traffic. The new 15·5-km long stretch of the "Autoroute du Leman" links Vevey with Rennaz, and passes through some of the most beautiful landscape in Europe. In addition to the engineering aspect, architectural factors received particular attention since Chillon Castle, a famous tourist attraction, had to be safeguarded. The motorway soars high above the castle along a boldly designed $2\frac{1}{2}$-km long viaduct which, supported by elegant columns, follows the contours of the mountain with its steep slope down to the lake. The new "European road of dreams" is being praised as one of the world's most beautiful panoramic highways.

3rd November: The picture above shows the U.S. President during an election meeting in
Phoenix, Arizona. Despite the unprecedented efforts for a mid-term election, made by President
Richard M. Nixon and his Vice-President Spiro T. Agnew, the Republicans failed to break
the Democrat's control of Congress. Although the Democrats suffered minor losses in the Senate,
where Nixon had concentrated his efforts, they remained the majority party. In the House of
Representatives they increased their dominance. The Republicans suffered serious losses but were
able to console themselves with the successful defence of their positions in the two most important
states of California and New York (where Nelson Rockefeller was re-elected for the fourth time,
thereby setting a new record). On the other hand, the Democrats' Edmund Muskie and Edward
Kennedy were returned to the Senate with large majorities and Hubert Humphrey who, as loser in
the 1968 Presidential Election had been driven from national politics, returned to the Capitol in
Washington. Another loser in 1968, George Wallace, the extreme right-wing third-party
candidate, also made a comeback being returned to the Governor's mansion in Alabama. The
candidates for the 1972 Presidential Elections were already taking up their starting positions.

Vice-President *Spiro T. Agnew*, the inexhaustible Republican campaigner, constantly reiterated the need for "law and order", but failed to offer any constructive solutions for the ills of a society in turmoil and clamoured for more police and law enforcement in the traditional style. This pugnacious politician was constantly involved in skirmishes with the mass media which resented his over-simplifications.

In California the Democratic candidate *John Tunney*, son of the former world boxing champion Gene Tunney, beat Senator George Murphy, who enjoyed the full backing of President Nixon. This victory was achieved despite the fact that he had been smeared as having incited campus rebels and bomb throwers.

The most astonishing victory was that won by 47-year-old Conservative *James L. Buckley* (on the right of the picture, with his brother *William F. Buckley*, whom John Lindsay once beat for the post of Mayor of New York City). He captured the Senate seat for New York which the liberal Republican Goodell has occupied since the assassination of Robert Kennedy and thus became the first third-party representative since 1940 to enter the Senate in Washington.

5th November: Peter II, Yugoslavia's last King, died at the age of 47 after a liver transplant in a Los Angeles hospital. A member of the Karageorgevich dynasty and great-grandson of Queen Victoria as well as Czar Alexander II, Crown Prince Peter was proclaimed King on 9th October 1934, after the assassination of his father, Alexander I, in Marseilles. The top picture shows the 14-year-old King whose powers had been transferred to a regent, inspecting his guards. King Peter only reigned for three weeks. Two days after Yugoslavia joined the Axis powers in March 1941, the monarchy was overthrown by a military coup and when Nazi troops marched in he was forced to flee the country. Exiled in London, he first supported the Serbian nationalist, Mihajlovic, but later, under pressure from Churchill gave his support to Tito's Communist Partisans. In 1945 he protested against the proclamation of Yugoslavia as a republic and was promptly deprived of his Yugoslav citizenship. Peter's only son, an officer in the British Army, declined to have himself crowned as "King in exile" after his father's death.

7th November: British Olympic athlete Lillian Board, aged 22, who had cancer of the stomach, went to Dr. Issels' Ringberg Clinic in Bavaria for treatment. Her condition worsened in the following few weeks and she was moved to Munich University Clinic for an emergency operation. She died on 26th December. The "golden girl of British Sport" never gave up hope of recovery, showing the same determination as she always showed at sport. Dr. Issels' clinic and controversial methods of treatment have been criticized by many medical experts.

6th November: All remained quiet on the armistice line dividing the Egyptians and Israelis along the Suez Canal after the officially agreed three months' armistice had expired. Both sides had let it be understood that they would not resume hostilities for the time being and would be prepared to have the armistice extended for a further three months. This enabled TV reporters to sit without cover and describe the scene along the most advanced Israeli positions on the bank of the canal. Nevertheless, Egypt made the extension of the armistice dependent upon the resumption of the Jarring talks, fearing that the armistice might become a *de facto* solution enabling the Israelis to remain in possession of the Arab territory they had occupied during the June war of 1967.

9th November: Thirteen days before his 80th birthday, General *Charles de Gaulle*, the saviour of France and her President for eleven years, died of a heart attack at his country seat "La Boisserie" at Colombey-les-Deux-Eglises in Lorraine. In the National Assembly the President of the Gaullist Party conveyed the sad news by saying: "My children, our father is dead". De Gaulle was the last of the grand old men of Europe; like very few European statesmen, he had had a hand in shaping modern history. President Pompidou, in a message to the French people, paid tribute to his predecessor: "In 1940 de Gaulle saved France's honour. In 1944 he led us to liberation and victory. In 1958 he saved us from civil war. He gave the Republic her institutions, her independence, and her place in the world." As early as 1952 the General had decreed in his will that he wanted to be buried in his village in Lorraine, without a state funeral. Neither President nor Ministers were to be at his graveside; only ordinary people and a detachment from the Armed Forces were to accompany him on his last journey. The great man's wish for a simple burial was respected: nevertheless, representatives of over a hundred nations, including 38 Heads of State, gathered for a Requiem Mass in the Cathedral of Notre Dame in Paris, to honour the man who had considered himself the incarnation of France. For one day Paris became what de Gaulle had always craved for, the political centre of the world. However, on that day the capital of France was 250 km away at the village of Colombey-les-Deux-Eglises with its 400 inhabitants.

An armoured car carried the coffin,
covered by the tricolour, from his
country seat "La Boisserie" to the
nearby village churchyard, where
Charles de Gaulle was interred at the
side of his beloved daughter, Anne,
who had died young. Tens of thousands
of people had gathered in the small
village to offer a last tribute to the
saviour of France.

The world took leave from General
de Gaulle by attending a Requiem Mass
in the Cathedral of Notre Dame in
Paris. Emperors, kings, presidents and
government representatives from more
than a hundred countries, including the
Presidents of the U.S.A. and the
U.S.S.R., attended the ceremony in the
venerable Gothic cathedral dating from
the 12th century.

Captain *Charles de Gaulle* in the fortress of
Ingolstadt in 1917, after he had been
badly wounded and taken prisoner by the
Germans during the bitter fighting for
Fort Douaumont at Verdun. He was
mentioned in despatches: "Captain
de Gaulle, known for his high intellectual
and moral valour, carried his men with
him into a furious attack at close quarters—
the only solution which he considered
compatible with his sense of military
honour."

50-year-old Brigadier-General *de Gaulle*
during his historic broadcast of 18th June
1940 in London, when he appealed to the
French people to continue the fight.
Two days later posters appeared in London
carrying the words: "France has lost a
battle. But France has not lost the war!
She will regain her liberty and her
greatness. That is my goal. That is why I
ask all Frenchmen, wherever they may be,
to unite with me in action, in sacrifice,
and in hope."

The Casablanca Conference in January 1943
agreed to force the Axis powers into
unconditional surrender. U.S. President
Franklin D. Roosevelt and Britain's Prime
Minister *Winston Churchill* tried to
mediate between the French rivals,
Henri Giraud and *Charles de Gaulle*.
Within a year the two-star General had
out-manoeuvred the five-star one.

A proud day in the life of de Gaulle:
on 26th August 1944, in liberated Paris,
the "Saviour of France" expresses his
gratitude to the armoured troops. The
French 2nd Armoured Division under
General Leclerc, together with their Allies,
had entered Paris. Seventeen months later
de Gaulle resigned as Head of the
Government and turned his back upon Paris.

The return to power: at a critical moment in French politics *de Gaulle* resumed governmental responsibilities by accepting the post of Prime Minister on 1st June 1958. He vigorously tackled the most pressing problem, that of North Africa. In Algiers, Europeans and Arabs gave him a tumultuous reception. He proclaimed to the roaring crowd: "Je vous ai compris." Five years later Algeria became independent.

From 1958 onwards President *de Gaulle* visited 37 countries and travelled about 300,000 km. The state visit to Canada in July 1967 had to be curtailed after he had made a speech from the balcony of Montreal town hall ending with the words "Vive le Quebec libre", the slogan of the French-Canadian separatists.

Return to solitude after relinquishing power: after the French people had rejected his plans for reforming the Senate and the regions, President *de Gaulle* resigned on the 28th April 1969. He withdrew from public life and lived quietly with his wife, *Yvonne*, at Colombey-les-Deux-Eglises, where he devoted himself to writing his memoirs.

Fleeing from hunger, thirst and disease, many survivors immediately left the disaster area carrying the few possessions they had been able to rescue from their devastated homes.

The most effective assistance was given by Britain. Four British naval vessels steamed from Singapore to the disaster area in the Ganges delta, bringing landing craft, 400 tons of food, water purification equipment, eight helicopters and 1,500 soldiers.

13th November: The Ganges estuary in East Pakistan was struck by the worst natural disaster of the century. Following a violent cyclone, a tidal wave 6 to 8 metres high swept across the flat coastal areas of the Bay of Bengal. It covered a wide strip of the coast and thirteen islands with a thick layer of mud and wiped 200 smaller islands off the map.
The area had not received adequate warning and people were caught literally in their beds by the tidal wave. Hundreds of thousands perished. The crews of the aircraft exploring the situation in the disaster area were confronted by a scene of utter devastation (top left-hand page, the flooded island of Bhola). Two and a half million people, who had survived the cyclone and the tidal wave, were faced with a protracted death by starvation and disease. The tragedy continued and thousands of men, women and children died every day, because the authorities of the Islamic state failed to take adequate relief measures. A single helicopter and a seaplane were assigned to rescue work. The gifts, which arrived in a steadily increasing flood from all parts of the globe, remained lying around at Dacca airport for weeks. On the island of Manapura, where 10,000 died, crowds of survivors surged round the first arrivals from the world outside, begging for food and water (left), seizing the hands of the rescuers and kissing their feet. Weeks elapsed before the military bureaucracy roused itself from its lethargy and relief began to be properly organized. The Central Government's failure in Islamabad, the capital, which is 2,000 km away from the disaster area, increased the existing tension between East and West Pakistan and strengthened the separatist tendencies in the East.

16th November: Nine weeks after landing the automatic moon probe Luna 16 on the moon's Sea of Fertility, Soviet space engineers achieved another sensational success. The moon probe Luna 17 deposited a mobile laboratory on the Mare Imbrium. An unmanned eight-wheeled moon crawler "Lunokhod 1", driven by eight electromotors built into its axles, rolled down a ramp from Luna 17 on to the lunar surface and set out on its journey of exploration. The moon crawler, which resembled a mobile soup tureen, was guided from the earth (the picture shows it during a test trip over difficult terrain on earth). It analysed rock samples in situ, carried out other research, and transmitted television pictures. The machinery of the moon crawler, which charged its batteries by solar cells, survived the tremendous stresses of heat and cold and resumed its journey after the lunar night.

20th November: The 1970 "Miss World" contest in London's Royal Albert Hall was troubled by an unexpected incident not normally associated with beauty contests. Militant supporters of the Women's Liberation Front threw smoke and stink bombs, leaflets and rotten fruit on to the stage and had to be forcibly ejected (below left). The winner was 22-year-old coloured *Jennifer Hosten*, an air hostess from Grenada, seen in the picture below the day after the contest, wearing her crown and walking round Grosvenor Square with a little Vietnamese girl. Her victory unleashed a political crisis in her native island in the West Indies. The opposition objected to the fact that the Prime Minister, Eric M. Gairy, who was a member of the "Miss World" jury, had travelled halfway round the world to assess the charms of a few curvaceous females and demanded a special session of the island's legislature.

21st November: A small helicopter-borne U.S. commando force made a bold attack on Son Tay prisoner-of-war camp 35 km west of Hanoi. The purpose of the raid was to liberate seventy American soldiers who, according to information from U.S. Intelligence sources, were being held prisoner in the camp. Simultaneous bombing raids, the first since May, were carried out by U.S. planes over North Vietnam to divert attention from the attack. The mission, code-named "Ivory Coast", was only partially successful; Son Tay camp was occupied without loss but the prisoners had been transferred several weeks earlier to another camp. Despite this failure, the raid was treated in Washington as a sensation and the leaders responsible were decorated by President Nixon. The picture shows Colonel *Arthur D. Simons* (left), who led the assault, giving a televised account. Others taking part in the programme were (from the left) Secretary of Defence *Melvin Laird*, Chairman of the Joint Chiefs of Staff, Admiral *Thomas Moorer*, and Brigadier *Leroy J. Manor*, the joint force commander of the raid. What the raid revealed was the lack of information on the adversary's military and political situation, a decisive weakness in the U.S. military operations in South-East Asia.

25th November: For one hour the mystical and imperialist past caught up with modern Japan. The famous novelist *Yukio Mishima*, protagonist of the romantic idea of a "purified empire" and of Japanese rearmament, together with four companions from his right-wing extremist "Tate No Kai" private army stormed a home-defence force headquarters in Tokyo, and tied the commanding General *Kanetoshi Mashita* to his chair. From the balcony of the headquarters Mishima then exhorted the 2,000 officers and men to rise against the Government and to change the constitution forced upon the country by the victors in the Second World War. Interrupted by heckling and booing from the soldiers, he terminated his appeal by shouting "Long live the Emperor!" and committed hara-kiri in front of the General. After Mishima had plunged the samurai-style sword into his body, his young second-in-command Masakazu Morita followed the ancient tradition by beheading him and then also committed ritual suicide. Top left, General Mashita after being untied is seen accompanied by an adjutant who had been wounded in the head during the fight with Mishima's followers. In addition to having trained an 87-strong private army in the spirit of the samurai virtues Mishima was one of Japan's most successful writers and a candidate for the Noble Prize for Literature.

27th November: The Pope's ninth trip abroad took him to Asia and Australia; it was not only his longest and most strenuous so far—but nearly his last. A few moments after his arrival at Manila airport, in the Philippines, an attempt on the life of Paul VI was only narrowly prevented. The 35-year-old Bolivian painter *Benjamin Mendoza y Amor* (below right, wearing glasses), who had succeeded in penetrating the barriers dressed as a priest, tried to assassinate the Pope (extreme left, partially hidden) with a dagger. However, he was overpowered, after Monsignor *Pasquale Macci*, Secretary to the Pope, had courageously thrown himself at the attacker. The picture, one of the most dramatic photographs of the year, records the moment when the Pope was looking straight at his attacker. When Mendoza, a surrealist painter, met the Press (right), he explained that he had been planning the attack for a long time and would be prepared to make another attempt any time "to save humanity from evil". The Pope, who was confronted in Manila not only by an assassin but also by festering slums, had embarked upon his long journey to attend two Bishops' conferences, an Asian one in Manila and an Australian/Polynesian one in Sydney. Further stages of the journey covering more than 45,000 km in ten days were Teheran, where Pope Paul VI met the Shah, Dacca in East Pakistan where he encouraged survivors of the flood disaster, Pago Pago on Samoa, Djakarta in Indonesia, Hong Kong where he praised Chinese wisdom and offered brotherly greetings to the 750 million Chinese, and Colombo in Ceylon.

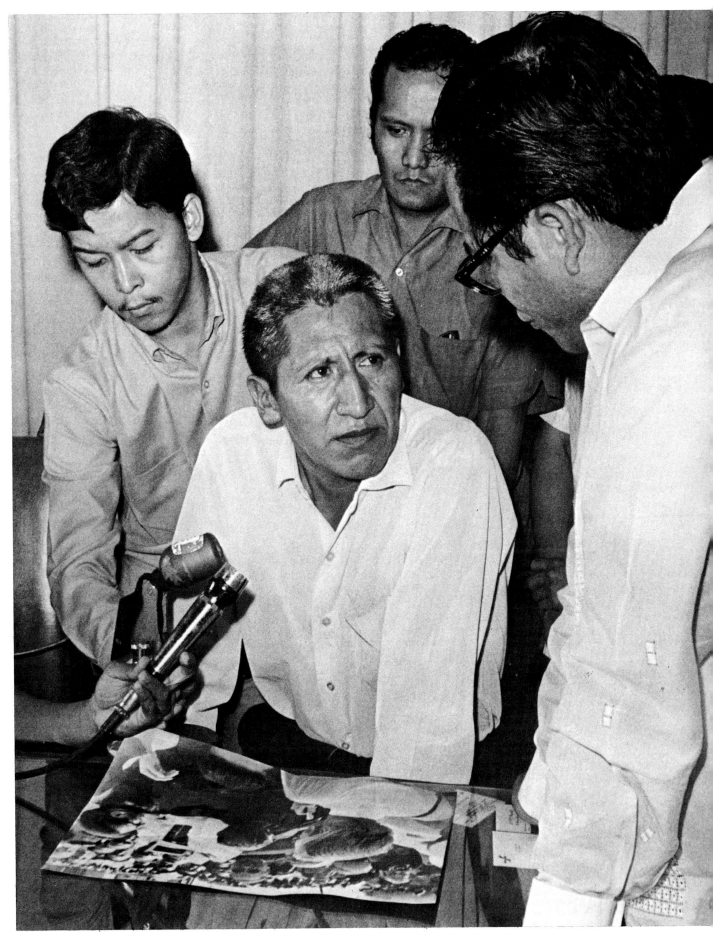

Nikita Khrushchev, the former Head of the Soviet Union and its most famous old-age pensioner, once more hit the headlines in November, when his alleged memoirs turned up in the West. They were acquired for publication by a number of journals and newspapers, including *The Times*. After his wife, *Nina*, had stated that this was "an error or a hoax", Khrushchev signed a declaration stating categorically that he had handed neither memoirs nor material suitable for memoirs to any foreign or Soviet publisher. He added that the whole thing was a forgery by the "corrupt bourgeois press". However, the declaration did not deny that he had written or dictated his memoirs. The subsequent rumours that the disowned "reminiscences" had been brought out of the U.S.S.R., by a member of the KGB, the Soviet secret service, only deepened the mystery surrounding the whole affair, causing widespread speculation.

Заявление

Как видно из сообщений печати Соединенных Штатов Америки и некоторых других капиталистических стран , в настоящее время готовятся к публикации так называемые мемуары или воспоминания Н.С.Хрущева. Это - фабрикация и я возмущен ею. Никаких мемуаров или материалов мемуарного характера я никогда никому не передавал - ни "Тайму", ни другим заграничным издательствам. Не передавал таких материалов я и советским издательствам. Поэтому я заявляю, что все это является фальшивкой. В такой лжи уже неоднократно уличалась продажная буржуазная печать.

Н.Хрущев

10/II-1920г

December

A new man rises to power in Poland after a rebellion by the people of the Baltic towns: *Edward Gierek*, the new Party Leader, is a technocrat.

World-wide protests against the savage sentences at Burgos and Leningrad: demonstration in West Berlin in support of the Basque separatists.

The chain of political eruptions in Eastern Europe (*East Berlin 1953, Budapest and Poznan 1956, Prague 1968*) gained a further link in December of 1970. Violent disorders broke out in Poland's Baltic cities as a result of massive price rises; in Gdansk and Szczecin, under the leadership of dockyard workers, they assumed the character of a real popular uprising. Although the workers' revolt was ruthlessly suppressed, it toppled the Polish leaders. Poland's worst crisis since 1956 was caused by the miserable economic situation. When Gomulka, the Party Leader, tried to deal with the effects of bad planning by drastic economic measures, the price increases he imposed caused popular indignation. The 1956 revolt by the workers of Poznan had restored him to power after he had been pushed aside by the Stalinists. But the resistance hero of the Second World War, who had then been welcomed as the saviour of the nation from misery and injustice, now finally lost his hold on power to Edward Gierek, the technocrat. Gomulka, who was no longer able to master the complicated mechanisms of a modern economy left office as a failure and a sick and embittered man.

The military court at Burgos, in Spain, was not only intended to try the 16 Basque men accused, but the whole ETA movement, and to intimidate the growing opposition by harsh sentences. But the show trial of the Basques turned more and more into a show trial of the régime which, 30 years after the end of the civil war, still has to rely on military courts and emergency laws. The brutal sentences and the wrangling about whether or not they should be carried out showed all the signs of an internal power struggle in which the contestants took up their positions for the post-Franco era. The military judges favouring justice by deterrent, an attitude rooted in the philosophy of the civil war, confronted the President with no fewer than three double death sentences. Refusal to accept them would inevitably appear as provocation of the armed forces. Against the bitter resistance of the hardliners, Franco saw himself nevertheless obliged to grant reprieves, since the carrying out of the sentences would have endangered the régime's foreign policy and created an extremely dangerous situation on the home front.

The second political trial of the month, that of a group of Jewish Soviet citizens accused of having planned the hijacking of an aircraft to Sweden, displayed the same characteristics of a show of power for internal reasons which was subsequently softened for the sake of foreign policy. As justification of the Leningrad death sentences the Soviet Union cited the international convention against hijacking, which had been signed at The Hague a few days earlier. After two Aeroflot planes had been hijacked to Turkey and the Turkish Government had refused to extradite the four hijackers, the U.S.S.R. suddenly showed considerable interest in the discussions which lead to the signing of this convention.

December 1 Italy's parliament passes first divorce law.
2 German Consul Eugen Beihl at San Sebastian kidnapped by Basque separatists.
3 Diplomat James Cross released in Montreal after two months as hostage. Kidnappers receive safe passage to Cuba.
7 Brandt and Cyrankiewicz sign German/Polish treaty in Warsaw.
Giovanni Enrico Bucher, Swiss Ambassador to Brazil, kidnapped by urban guerrillas.
Pakistan general election results in landslide victory for Sheikh Mujibur Rahman's Awami League in East Pakistan, and for Zulfikar Ali Bhutto's People's Party in West Pakistan.
8 U.N. Security Council condemns Portugal for involvement in Guinea invasion.
9 Prosecution in Basque trial at Burgos demands death sentences against six of the accused.
14 Violent disorders in Poland's Baltic cities of Gdansk, Szczecin, Gdynia, Sopot, Slupsk and Elblag.
Death of Field-Marshal Viscount Slim, aged 79.
15 303 killed in Korean ferry disaster.
16 International convention against hijacking signed at The Hague.

20 Shift in power in Poland: Party Leader Wladyslaw Gomulka replaced by Edward Gierek.
23 Josef Cyrankiewicz resigns as Polish Premier and becomes President. Piotr Jaroszewicz, hitherto his Deputy, becomes Prime Minister.
Régis Debray pardoned and expelled from Bolivia.
24 Consul Beihl released by ETA.
Soviet Jews accused of planning hijacking receive death sentences and long periods of imprisonment in Leningrad trial.
28 Military court at Burgos pronounces nine death sentences against six Basques. Nine accused sentenced to prison sentences ranging from six to 72 years.
Israeli Cabinet approves resumption of Jarring talks.
Arrest of suspected assassins of Minister Laporte in Canada.
30 Franco reprieves the Basques sentenced to death.
31 Leningrad death sentences commuted to 15 years each in corrective labour colonies.

3rd December: Two months after the kidnapping of the British diplomat, *James Cross*, by members of the "Quebec Liberation Front", police in Montreal tracked down the hideout of the abductors and surrounded it. At first the kidnappers threatened to blow themselves up with their hostage but later offered to release the diplomat in exchange for a safe passage to Cuba. Premier Trudeau accepted the condition. After the three FLQ terrorists and members of their families had been flown to Havana in a Canadian Air Force plane, Cross was set free by the Cuban Consul who had been acting as an intermediary. The picture shows Cross, with his wife *Barbara*, describing his experiences in London.

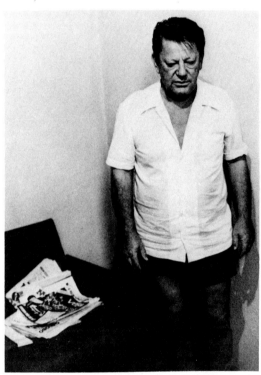

7th December: The fourth kidnapping of a foreign diplomat by members of the underground took place in Brazil. 57-year-old *Giovanni Enrico Bucher*, the Swiss Ambassador, was attacked by the "Juarez Guimaraes de Brito" commando of the "Revolutionary People's Vanguard" (VPR) on his way from his residence to the Embassy. Bucher's large black car was stopped in the Rua Conde de Baependi by a car drawn across the road (bottom picture) and the diplomat was dragged by a group of heavily armed guerrillas into another vehicle. A Brazilian security guard, who offered resistance, was shot down. The terrorists left leaflets signed by the "National Liberation Alliance" (ALN) in which, for the first time, foreign diplomats in Brazil were openly accused of collaboration with the "dictatorship by looters, exploiters, torturers and murderers". In return for Bucher's release his kidnappers demanded the release of 70 political prisoners, the publication by the mass media of the manifestoes left behind by the "Liberation Alliance", and the disclosure of Brazilian bank accounts in Switzerland by the Swiss Government. Ten thousand policemen and soldiers made a fruitless search for the kidnappers who photographed their hostage in their hiding place (left) and sold the picture to foreign newspapers. Negotiations were slow and Bucher had to spend New Year's Eve in the company of his kidnappers.

7th December: This picture, which is evidence of the efforts by *Willy Brandt*, the Federal German Chancellor, for reconciliation with the East, was widely considered the "picture of the year 1970". Before signing the German-Polish treaty as the "basis for normalizing mutual relations", the core of which is Bonn's recognition of the Oder-Neisse line as Poland's western frontier, the Chancellor laid a wreath at the memorial for the victims of the revolt of the Warsaw ghetto in 1943 and then, in a spontaneous gesture of humility, went down on his knees in memory of the Jews slaughtered by Hitler's butchers. It was a successful initial approach to the problem of breathing life into the Warsaw treaty which was to set the pace for a new relationship between Poles and Germans. Foreign Ministers Scheel and Jedrychowski had agreed upon large-scale repatriation of Polish citizens of German origin to the Federal Republic during their negotiations.

10th December: Dr. *Norman Ernest Borlaug*, the 56-year-old U.S. agricultural scientist and "father of the green revolution", received the 1970 Nobel Prize for Peace, worth 500,000 Norwegian crowns, in Oslo. He had been in charge of a group of scientists from 17 different countries who had evolved entirely new strains of high-yield grain at the International Maize and Wheat Improvement Centre in Mexico City, thereby making an extremely important contribution to the abolition of hunger throughout the world. In the absence of Alexander Solzhenitsyn, the award winner for Literature, the following received their Nobel Prizes in Stockholm: Ulf von Euler (Sweden), Sir Bernard Katz (Britain) and Julius Axelrod (United States) for Medicine; Luis Leloir (Argentina) for Chemistry; Hannes Alfvén (Sweden) and Louis Néel (France) for Physics; and Paul A. Samuelson (United States) for Economics.

7th December: The result of the election for a new Constituent Assembly in Pakistan was a political landslide. 49-year-old Sheikh *Mujibur Rahman*, heading the Awami League, which favours autonomy for East Pakistan, gained an absolute majority in the new parliament and had every right to expect that, as Prime Minister of the Muslim republic, he would preside over a return to democracy.

14th December: Dramatic increases of around 20 per cent in prices of food, textiles and fuel triggered off a popular uprising in Poland's Baltic cities of Gdansk, Szczecin, Gdynia, Slupsk and Elblag. Although the revolt was ruthlessly suppressed by police and soldiers, it brought about a decisive change in the leadership in Warsaw and terminated the Gomulka era. Party and Government merely blamed young hoodlums, who "had nothing in common with the working class" for the disorders. In reality it was a workers' revolt started by the workers of the dockyards in Gdansk: they organized themselves democratically, formed strike committees and dockyard militias and confidently opposed the all-powerful Party by elected spokesmen who voiced not only economic but also political demands. After units of the militia had tried to stop the strikers marching to the Party headquarters and panicky police had fired into the crowd, popular anger exploded and spread to other coastal towns. There were acts of revenge against the forces of law and order and looting (below left the looting of a clothing shop in Gdansk; right the burning Party building in Szczecin). Prime Minister Cyrankiewicz authorized police and troops to use fire-arms. The Government, afraid that the revolt might spread to other parts of the country, ordered the area to be cut off and sent armoured units to suppress the disorders. According to reliable sources, these measures caused some 60 deaths and hundreds of injured. Despite their violent reaction, the men in power in Warsaw were unable to withstand the force of the gale from the Baltic and a complete reshuffle took place within the Government and the Party leadership.

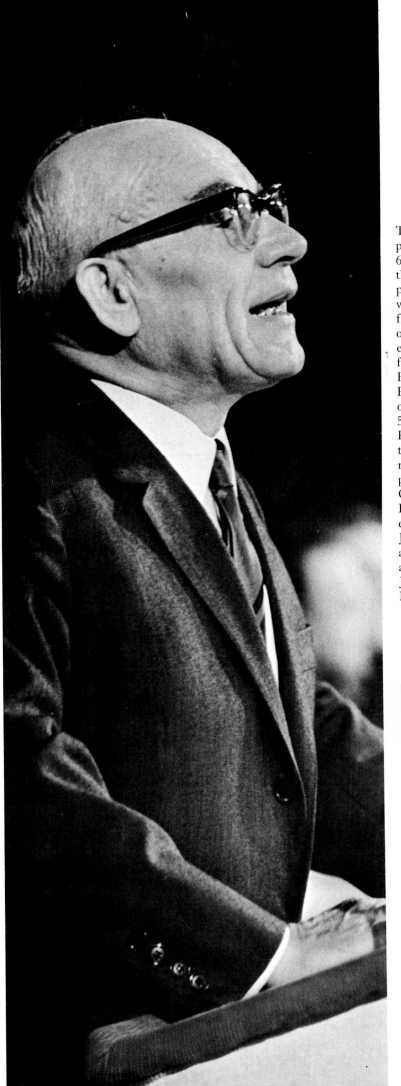

The most prominent victim of the popular uprising in Poland was 65-year-old *Wladyslaw Gomulka* (left), the Party Leader, who had come to power in 1956 as a result of the workers' riots at Poznan and now fell from power after workers had rioted once more. After his fall Gomulka entered a hospital to undergo treatment for a circulatory ailment and eye trouble. His successor as First Secretary of the Polish United Workers' Party (the name of the Communist Party in Poland) was 57-year-old *Edward Gierek*, until then Party Secretary in Silesia. In an appeal to the nation, he promised a re-examination of the new five-year plan. The technocrat Gierek is the first Communist Party Leader in Eastern Europe to have spent 20 years as an emigrant in the West. Prime Minister Josef Cyrankiewicz became President, a post vacated by Marian Spychalski, a supporter of Gomulka. Piotr Jaroszewicz, until then Deputy Prime Minister, was appointed Premier.

28th December: The trial of 16 Basque nationalists by the Franco régime before the military court at Burgos caused tension in Spain and passionate sympathy for the young accused in the rest of the world. They were accused of having been responsible, as members and sympathizers of the militant Marxist separatist movement ETA ("Basque Country and Freedom"), for the killing of Militon Manzanas, the head of the political police in Guipozcoa Province, and of being involved in banditry, terror and other crimes. While the military judges at Burgos deliberated upon the verdict for 19 days, the Government responded to the wave of demonstrations at home and abroad by organizing mass demonstrations and 100,000 people in Madrid shouted slogans demanding punishment for the guilty Basques. Speaking from the balcony of the National Palace in Madrid, Generalissimo *Francisco Franco* (the picture right shows his designated successor *Juan Carlos* and his wife *Sophie* behind Franco) addressed the crowd: "Words fail me in the face of this support for the unity of our country and the path of our nation. It is because we have a state based on law, our constitution and our basic laws, that we also have the solution of all problems." The picture below shows Basques on hunger strike at the San Antonio Church in Bilbao, singing the ancient martial songs of their people. Although the West German Consul at San Sebastian, *Eugen Beihl*, who had been kidnapped by an ETA splinter group on 2nd December, had been released without any *quid pro quo* four days before the announcement of the verdict (top left the 59-year-old hostage with his wife and daughter after his release), the judges imposed very harsh sentences, despite the lack of convincing evidence. Six of the accused were sentenced to death, three of them receiving double death sentences, and nine others received up to 72 years in prison. As a result of world-wide indignation and the intervention of many foreign Heads of State and governments (Pope Paul VI phoned the Spanish President to plead for clemency) Franco reprieved the Basques sentenced to death two days later, commuting their sentences to prison terms of 30 years.

The six Basques sentenced to death and subsequently reprieved by Franco, in Burgos prison (left): 29-year-old printer *Francisco Javier Izco*, 25-year-old student *Eduardo Uriarte*, 26-year-old mechanic *Joaquin Gorostidi*, 22-year-old mechanic *Mario Onaindia*, 25-year-old student *Francisco Javier Larena*, and 29-year-old teacher *José Maria Dorronsoro*. Franco's act of clemency defused the most explosive crisis which had occurred in Spain since the end of the civil war.

Bolivia's new President, Juan José Torres, granted an amnesty to 30-year-old *Régis Debray*, the French revolutionary writer, at Christmas. Debray had been sentenced in 1967, by a military court in Camiri, to 30 years in prison for his part in "Che" Guevara's jungle rebellion. After his release Debray, the son of a Paris millionaire, settled down as press adviser to President Allende of Chile.

31st December: The day after the reprieve of the six Basques there followed the reprieve of two Soviet Jews, Eduard Kuznetsov and Mark Dymshits, who had been sentenced to death for hijacking at a trial in Leningrad. These death sentences also caused world-wide reactions, particularly in Israel. Mass demonstrations demanded the unhindered departure of fellow Jews from the Soviet Union (below). The Court of Appeal in Moscow commuted the death sentences to 15 years each in corrective labour colonies.

Sports

Sportsman of the year: Brazil's star forward *Pelé* after his team's victory in the final of the World Cup football competition in Mexico City, where Brazil gained the greatly sought-after Jules Rimet Cup for the third time.

The principal sports event of 1970 was the final four rounds of the 9th World Cup football competition which took place in four Mexican cities. The final between Brazil and Italy in the Aztec Stadium in Mexico City became a brilliant display of aggressive football by the Brazilians who won the Cup for the third time, and will now keep it. European soccer was impressively represented particularly by Italy, Germany and England. Gerd Müller was the most successful scorer, but it was Pelé, the Brazilian, who was chosen sportsman of the year by the international sporting press. Eddy Merckx, the Belgian cyclist, won the Tour de France for the second time and also the Tour of Italy. Once more the most successful motor cyclist was Italy's Giacomo Agostini, unbeaten in world championship races since 1967.

The racing driver Jochen Rindt of Austria, who was involved in a fatal crash at Monza, was declared the first posthumous world champion. He had already collected so many points that no one could beat him.

1970 was also a year which saw brilliant records in athletics, such as the sensational times of Chi Cheng, the sprinter and hurdler from Nationalist China who was chosen sportswoman of the year, the high jump of Ni Chih Chin of the Chinese People's Republic who raised Valeri Brumel's world record by 1cm to 2·29m, and the incredible pole-vault of Christos Papanicolaou of Greece who raised the record by 3cm to 5·49m. The 9th Commonwealth Games were held in Edinburgh, where Scotland's middle distance runners gained great victories over the favourites.

A veritable avalanche of records at the European championships in Barcelona showed that swimming has made tremendous progress in Europe.

Disappointment was in store for those who expected the traditional fierce contest between Japan and the Soviet Union at the world gymnastics championship at Ljubljana: the Japanese gymnasts unequivocally dominated the competition.

On the other hand in the Nordic world ski championships in the High Tatra, the Soviet competitors were more successful than ever before, while eight skiers belonging to five nations shared eight gold medals in the Alpine championship at Val Gardena.

1970 was also the year in which the young Belgian Jean-Pierre Monséré, during the first year of his career as a professional road racer, shot right to the top and became world cycling champion. And it was in 1970 that David Broome, after winning three European championships, became world show jumping champion, Ard Schenk of the Netherlands became world speed skating champion, John Newcombe and Margaret Court, both Australians, triumphed at Wimbledon, Cassius Clay staged his come-back in boxing, Tony Jacklin won the U.S. Open Golf Championship, Henry Cooper regained his European Heavyweight title and the new British Prime Minister, Edward Heath, was voted Yachtsman of the Year. Exciting cricket was seen in a series of matches against a Rest of the World XI, after anti-apartheid feelings had caused the cancellation of the Test series against South Africa. Finally the year ended on a tragic note with the death through cancer of Lillian Board, aged 22, one of Britain's most dedicated athletes.

Ard Schenk of Holland became the fastest speed skater of the year. This 25-year-old medical student, who won the 1966 European championship, once more gained the title at Innsbruck and then went on to become world champion at the Bislet stadium at Oslo, where he beat the Norwegian Magne Thomassen and his fellow-Dutchman Kees Verkerk.

The 1970 world ski championships were held at Val Gardena, in Italy (Alpine events) and in the High Tatra, in Czechoslovakia (Nordic events) in ideal conditions. Some of the gold medals went to favourites but, in a number of cases, outsiders confirmed the saying about the "glorious uncertainty of sport". While the Soviet skiers dominated events in Czechoslovakia, to the audible displeasure of the public, the "scatter" of the gold medals at Val Gardena (eight skiers from five different countries shared the world titles) proved that there was little to choose between the participants in the Alpine events.

One of the most successful competitors in the Nordic ski championship at Strbske Pleso was the Russian *Vyacheslav Vedenin*, who beat the East German Gerhard Grimmer and the Norwegian Odd Martinsen to become world champion in the 30km race, and gained the silver medal in the 50km race.

34-year-old *Kalevi Oikarainen* won Finland's only gold medal in this Nordic ski championship with a terrific performance in the 50km race. His fellow-countrymen, in accordance with Scandinavian tradition, gave him a rousing welcome after his victory.

After many "lean" years Sweden once more succeeded in producing a world champion: 25-year-old *Lars-Göran Aslund* won a convincing victory over the Norwegian Odd Martinsen and the Russian Fedor Simasov in the 15km race.

The big surprise at the World Ski Championship in the High Tatra was the performance of 21-year-old Soviet ski-jumper *Gari Napalkov*, who became double world champion. He beat the Japanese Yukio Kasaya and the Norwegian Lars Grini on the ordinary ski-jump and then beat all the favourites with a record leap of 109·5m from the large ski-jump; Jiri Raska (CSSR) and Daniel Gasienica (Poland) had to be satisfied with second and third place. Filled with joy at his second victory, Napalkov threw his arms in the air. He had gained two of the seven gold medals which the Soviet competitors took home from Czechoslovakia.

21-year-old *Annerösli Zryd* of Switzerland won a sensational victory in the downhill race at Val Gardena. This farmer's daughter from Adelboden had been dogged by bad luck in her sports career. Suffering from bad pains in the back after an accident in gymnastics, she had been undergoing orthopaedic treatment but this did not prevent her from taking part in the race in which she reached a speed of 83·655km/h. She beat the world's best downhill racers, including Isabelle Mir of France, and thereby gained Switzerland's first world ski title for ten years. Despite her youth, the Swiss girl retired from active sport after her success.

In contrast to the downhill race there was a clear victory by the favourite, 21-year-old *Ingrid Lafforgue* of France, in the ladies' Slalom. Daughter of a famous Franco-Swedish family of skiers, she won a decisive victory in the struggle between France and the United States, by beating Barbara Cochran of the U.S.A. Bronze medallist Michèle Jacot, who also gained the world championship in the combination, completed the French triumph.

The men's downhill race turned out to be equally sensational. 21-year-old *Bernhard Russi* of Switzerland (top of left-hand page), with an average speed of 93·370km, beat Karl Cordin of Austria by 16 hundredths of a second and became world champion. A draftsman by profession, the young Swiss was not internationally known before the race. The picture above shows him surrounded by reporters.

Eight years after his first world championship victory at Chamonix *Karl Schranz* of Austria won another gold medal by beating his fellow-Austrian, the 23-year-old *Werner Bleiner* (right) and 29-year-old *Dumeng Giovanoli* of Switzerland (left) in the giant Slalom.

No. 11 turned out to be lucky for *Jean-Noel Augert* of France. He was the surprise winner in the Slalom, while his fellow-countryman *Patrick Russell* (right), the favourite, had to be content with the silver medal. The bronze medal went to 27-year-old *Billy Kidd* of the United States (left) who also secured the title of world champion in the Combination.

21-year-old *Gabriele Seyfert* of East Germany successfully defended her title in the world figure skating championship at Ljubljana, in Yugoslavia, following her win in the European championship in Leningrad. This great figure skater was competing for the last time. The other world figure skating champions of 1969, the Russians Rodnina/Ulanov for pairs and the American Tim Wood for the men's event, kept their titles in 1970.

In the World Gymnastics Championship for women, which also took place at Ljubljana, in Yugoslavia, the Russian team beat the East German into second place. The winner in the Octathlon was the Russian Ludmilla Turitcheva who beat Erika Zuchold of East Germany.

The World Ice-Hockey tournament
of 1970 was not a happy one. After
the International Ice-Hockey
Federation, under pressure from the
International Olympic Committee,
had reversed its decision to permit
the inclusion of up to seven
professionals in each world
tournament team, the Canadians and
Americans withdrew. The
tournament, which was to have taken
place in Canada, had to be
transferred to Stockholm. As
expected, the Soviet Union won their
tenth world title, the eighth in a row.
The Czechs, who were the Russians'
most redoubtable opponents, fielded a
team which was visibly weaker than
that of the year before. There were
surprise victories by Finland over the
CSSR and Sweden.

Sweden beat the Soviet Union 4–2 in
the first round of the Stockholm
tournament. Above a scene from this
enjoyable match in which Sweden's
goalkeeper *Leif "Honken" Holmqvist*
proved a tower of strength.

The picture shows one of the Soviet
team falling, during their game with
Finland. The Finns, known as the
"giant killers", were soundly beaten
by the Soviet Union 16–1.

The matches between the Soviet Union and the CSSR, fought with great courage and competence, had been among the most exciting events of 1969. All the Czechs achieved in their two matches against the Russians in 1970 was one goal per match (their jubilation after one of them is shown above). The Russians, on the other hand, scored a total of eight goals. The disconsolate Czech goalkeeper is shown on the left.

One of the most successful sportswomen of the year was 26-year-old athlete *Chi Cheng* from
Formosa, who has been studying in California since 1963. At the 1968 Olympic Games in
Mexico City she had won a bronze medal in the 80m hurdles; in 1970 she reached her peak.
Her hour of triumph came at Portland (U.S.A.) when she lowered the world record for the
220yds. to 22·5 seconds (picture) and ran the 100 yds. in the new world record time of
10 seconds. The following month she achieved a new world record time of 22·4 seconds for the
200m in Munich and equalled another world record by running the 100m hurdles in
12·8 seconds.

The Europeans replaced the Americans, who have been the uncontested leaders in the pole-
vault for many years. The East German Wolfgang Nordwig broke John Pennel's world record
of 5·44m by 1cm in East Berlin and later in Turin reached 5·46m. Then 28-year-old *Christos
Papanicolaou* of Greece, who had never had much success at any of the big championships,
improved the world record by no less than 3cm at home in Athens reaching 5·49m, one of
the year's most outstanding athletic achievements.

Once more the Wimbledon final, despite the premature elimination of Rod Laver, the favourite, was an all-Australian affair. 26-year-old *John Newcombe* (above right) won this unofficial world tennis championship, for the second time since 1967. He beat the nine years older *Ken Rosewall* (on the left of the picture above left) who, in this dramatical and beautifully played match, failed for the third time with victory almost within his grasp. It was the first men's final since 1949 which required five sets (5–7, 6–3, 6–2, 3–6, 6–1).

Cassius Clay alias *Muhammad Ali*, the former world boxing champion, who had been banned from boxing and deprived of his world title after his conviction for refusing to do his military service, celebrated a brilliant come-back by beating the white Californian, *Jerry Quarry*, by a technical knock-out in the third round of their fight at Atlanta (picture). Later Clay had rather more trouble with Oscar Bonavena of Argentina whom he did not manage to knock out until the last of the fifteen rounds. His win cleared the way for the world title fight against Joe Frazier.

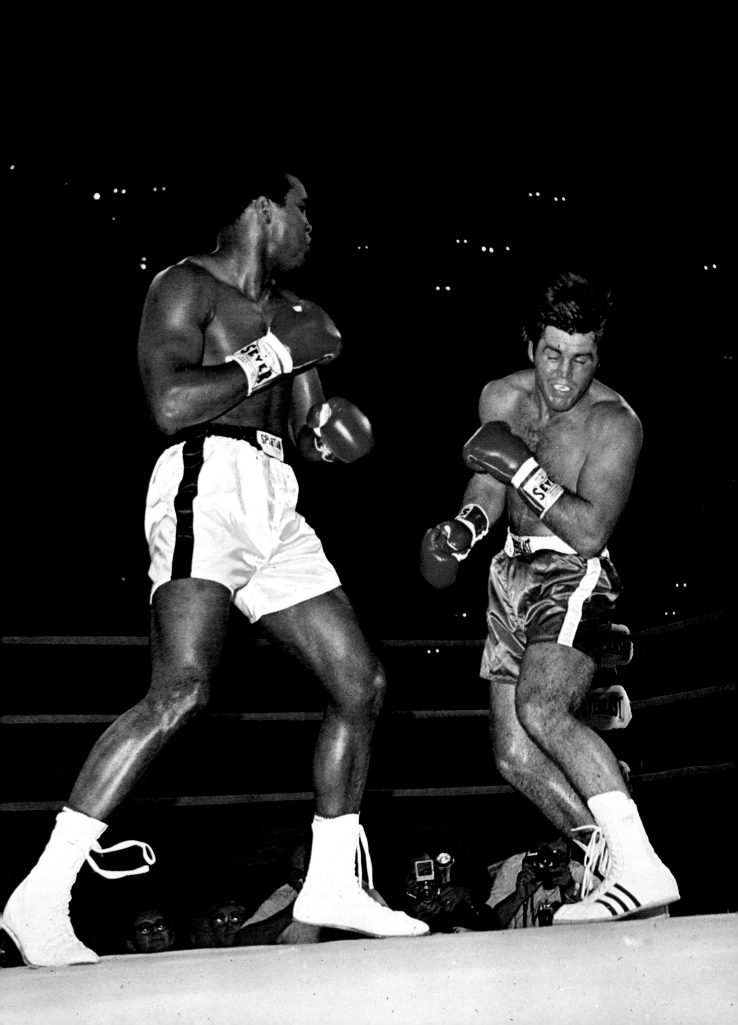

Giacomo Agostini, the Italian who had remained unbeaten in world championship races since 1967, once more became world motor cycle champion in the 350cc class and the 500cc class. He inspired millions of spectators by his elegant style.

The leading cyclist of 1970 was once again *Eddy Merckx*. Not only was the 25-year-old Belgian the winner of the Tour de France for the second time and of eight of the Tour's stages, but he also avenged his controversial disqualification in the 1969 Tour of Italy, when he won in great style this year. He also came first in dozens of big and small races; the only title he did not achieve was that of world champion.

The swimmers at the European
championship in Barcelona notched up a
staggering number of records. The Picornell
Stadium in Barcelona was the scene of six
new world records, 29 European records
and 29 national records. The most
successful competitor was the blond Swede,
19-year-old *Gunnar Larsson* (above), who
became triple European champion and
established two new world records, 4:02·6
for the 400m free style and 2:09·3 for the
200m medley. In the 400m medley he
achieved a new European record of 4:36·2.
Larsson, who had been a student in the
United States, had profited a great deal
from American training methods.

The picture above shows the new European
diving champion, *Giorgio Cagnotto* of Italy.

Mexico, where the final round of the 9th World Cup football competition started on 31st May, became the centre of attention. Seventy-one of the 135 national associations affiliated to the International Federation of Association Football (FIFA) had sent their teams to take part in the qualifying rounds, of which 14 had qualified for the final round: Belgium, Brazil, Bulgaria, Germany, El Salvador, Israel, Italy, Morocco, Peru, Rumania, Sweden, the Soviet Union, Czechoslovakia and Uruguay, plus England, the defenders of the title, and Mexico, the hosts. After England, in a dramatic contest, had been eliminated by Germany in the quarter-finals, four former world champions clashed in the semi-finals: Brazil, Germany, Italy and Uruguay. Germany, in a memorable match, was narrowly beaten by Italy after extra time. Brazil experienced less trouble in beating Uruguay. The final thus became a confrontation between Italy, world champions of 1930 and 1934, and Brazil, world champions of 1958 and 1962. The South American favourites achieved a clear 4–1 victory over the Italians, who were still suffering from their exhausting semi-final. To the delight of the South Americans, Brazil took final possession of the gold Jules Rimet Cup. The German team secured third place by their narrow 1–0 defeat of Uruguay.

This shot (left) by *Gerd Müller*, the German centre forward, in the 108th minute of the quarter-final between Germany and England at Leon Stadium spelt doom for the title holders. England gained a lead of 2–0; then after ninety minutes the score was levelled at 2–2. England's goalkeeper, *Peter Bonetti*, was powerless in the face of Müller's shot that decided the match. "Bomber" Müller, with ten goals to his credit, was the most successful scorer of this final round.

The semi-final between Italy and Germany, the "match of the century", also spilled over into extra time. After full-back *Karl-Heinz Schnellinger* had out-manoeuvred *Enrico Albertosi*, Italy's goalkeeper, during the last seconds of normal time, and scored the equalizer for Germany (below right), a goal by Rivera in the 112th minute decided the match (4–3). The breathtaking and dramatic game was fought by both teams with utter determination (the picture below left shows *Franz Beckenbauer* and *Sandro Mazzola* fighting for the ball).

The final game of the 9th World Cup competition between Brazil and Italy was held in the impressive Aztec Stadium in Mexico City, filled with 112,000 spectators. The enterprising and versatile forwards of Brazil, trained by Mario Zagallo, their national coach, repeatedly shattered Italy's dreaded tough defences (the picture below shows *Jairzinho* and *Pelé* in an encounter with full-backs *Giacinto Facchetti* and *Tarcisio Burgnich*) and scored no fewer than four goals (by Pelé, Gerson, Jairzinho and Carlos Alberto), whilst the Italians failed to exploit the weaknesses of Brazil's unimpressive rearguard and only achieved a consolation goal, scored by Boninsegna. Brazil provided the best team of this World Cup competition and deserved to win. The gold Jules Rimet Cup, donated in 1930 by the then FIFA President and bearing his name, has now been won by Brazil three times and will remain there for good. This success is closely linked with the name of Pelé, the brilliant 30-year-old forward who played for the Brazilian team as long ago as the World Cup in Stockholm in 1958. This was his third World Cup win. In the 1970 final he was the most outstanding player in the victorious team.

The picture left shows the Brazilians making things hot for the Italian defence. *Rivelino* has broken through and cannot be stopped.

Below left: the spell is broken in the 18th minute of the final. Pelé, full of joy, has scored for the first time by heading the ball into the Italian goal.

Carlos Alberto, Brazil's Captain, who himself scored one of the goals, shows the World Cup to the cheering crowd.

The 9th Commonwealth Games took place at the specially constructed new Meadowbank Stadium in Edinburgh. The top three medal winners were:

	Gold	Silver	Bronze
Australia	36	24	22
England	27	25	32
Canada	18	24	24

Above left: the double triumph for Scotland in the 5000 metres final. *Ian Stewart* breasts the tape to win in a new U.K. all-comers and Games record time. Second is compatriot *Ian McCafferty*. Third was the favourite, Kenya's *Kipchoge Keino*.

Above right: *J. L. Stewart* (Scotland), lying third in the picture, was the surprise winner of the 10,000 metres final. Ron Clarke (Australia 11) was second and R. Taylor (England 130) was third.

The picture below shows *Sylvia Potts* (New Zealand) falling one stride away from the finishing line of the 1500 metres Women's Final, when victory was almost certainly hers. Finishing first is *Rita Ridley* (England 472) with *Joan Page* (England 469) second and *T. Fynn* (Canada 432) third.

After the cancellation of the visit of the South African cricket team following the threats of disruption of matches and demonstrations over the policy of apartheid, a series of three matches was arranged between England and the Rest of the World. The winners were the Rest of the World by two matches to one. In the second of these Test matches, *Colin Cowdrey* broke the late Walter Hammond's record for the highest number of runs made in Test Cricket. He is seen here in confident style hitting bowler Gary Sobers for two runs.

David Broome, riding "Mister Softee", won the Men's European Show Jumping Championship held at Hickstead in Sussex. He crowned this success by winning the Men's World Show Jumping Championship held at La Baule, France, riding "Beethoven".

Lester Piggott won the Derby riding "Nijinsky" owned by the American industrialist Charles Englehard. This was Piggott's fifth Derby win and the eighth successive race won by "Nijinsky". However, this was the end of his series of wins for in his next two races he was beaten. The picture shows "Nijinsky" in the lead from "Gyr" (Bill Williamson) second and "Stintino" (Gerald Thiboeuf) third, partly hidden behind "Gyr".

The winner of the Grand National was "Gay Trip" owned by A. J. Chambers and ridden by 40-year-old Pat Taaffe. He is seen in the picture clearing the last fence.

The European heavyweight boxing title was regained by *Henry Cooper* at the Empire Pool, Wembley, when he beat the defending champion *Jose Urtain* of Spain. The fight was stopped by the referee at the beginning of the ninth round after Urtain had sustained severe cuts and his right eye was almost closed with swelling. Cooper had unleashed a stream of lefts to his face in the seventh and eighth rounds.

The Fijian Rugby Team visited Britain for a short tour and won much admiration for their open and attacking play. They played 14 matches, won six, drew one and lost seven for an aggregate of 168 points against 163 points. Before every match they performed their war dance or "Cibi" and the Maori valedictory song "Now is the Hour" was sung. The picture shows a loose maul in their match against London Counties at Twickenham, which they lost.

British Sporting Achievements

Athletics

World Records

4 × 800 m Women's Relay (8 min 27 sec): Rosemary Stirling, Sheila Carey, Pat Lowe, Lillian Board
4 × 700 m Women's Relay (8 min 25 sec): Rosemary Stirling, Sheila Carey, Pat Lowe, Georgina Craig
39 km (1 hr 31 min 30·4 sec): James Alder

Commonwealth Games Winners

MEN: 5,000 Metres: I. Stewart (Scotland) (European, U.K. and Games record); 10,000 Metres: I. Stewart (Scotland); 110 Metres Hurdles: D. Hemery (England); 400 Metres Hurdles: J. Sherwood (England); Marathon: R. Hill (England) (European, U.K. and Games best time); Pole Vault: M. Bull (N. Ireland); Long Jump: L. Davies (Wales); Hammer: H. Payne (England); Javelin: D. Travis (England)

WOMEN: 800 Metres: R. Stirling (Scotland); 1,500 Metres: R. Ridley (England); Long Jump: S. Sherwood (England); Shot: M. Peters (N. Ireland); Discus: R. Payne (Scotland); Pentathlon: M. Peters (N. Ireland)

Boxing

World Title

Lightweight: Ken Buchanan

European Titles

Heavyweight: Henry Cooper; Welterweight: Ralph Charles

British Titles

Heavyweight: Henry Cooper; Light-Heavyweight: Eddie Avoth; Middleweight: Bunny Sterling; Welterweight: Ralph Charles; Lightweight: Ken Buchanan; Featherweight: Jimmy Revie; Bantamweight: Alan Rudkin; Flyweight: John McCluskey

Cricket

England v. Rest of World

First Test: England 127 and 339; Rest of World 546. Rest of World won by 80 runs

Second Test: Rest of World 276 and 286; England 279 and 284 for 2. England won by 8 wickets

Third Test: England 294 and 409; Rest of World 563 for 9 dec and 141 for 5. Rest of World won by 5 wickets

Australia v. England

First Test: Australia 433 and 214; England 464 and 39 for 1. Match drawn

Second Test: England 397 and 287 for 6 dec; Australia 440 and 100 for 3. Match drawn

The remaining four Tests to be played in 1971

The County Champions were Kent

The Gillette Cup winners were Lancashire

Football

Home Internationals

N. Ireland 0, Scotland 1; Wales 1, England 1; England 3, N. Ireland 1; Scotland 0, Wales 0; Wales 1, N. Ireland 0; Scotland 0, England 0

F.A. Cup: Chelsea; F.A. Amateur Cup: Enfield; Football League Champions: Everton; Football League Cup Winners: Manchester City; Scottish League Champions: Celtic; Friars Cup: Arsenal

Golf

U.S. Open Championship: Tony Jacklin
British Amateur Championship: Michael Bonallack; English Championship: Dr. David Marsh; Long John Scotch Whisky P.G.A. Championship: Tommy Horton; Wills Open Championship: Tony Jacklin; Home International Championship: Scotland

Hockey

Home Counties Tournament

England 1, Scotland 2; England 2, Wales 0; England 0, Wales 0; Scotland 0, Ireland 0; Scotland 0, Wales 0; Ireland 2, Wales 1

International Matches

England 0, Pakistan 1; England 1, Spain 1; England 1, France 0

Horse Racing

The Derby: Nijinsky (Lester Piggott); The Oaks: Lupe (Sandy Barclay); St. Leger: Nijinsky (Lester Piggott); 2000 Guineas: Nijinsky (Lester Piggott); 1000 Guineas: Humble Duty (Lester Piggott); Ascot Gold Cup: Precipice Wood (Jimmy Lindley); Grand National: Gay Trip (Pat Taaffe); Cheltenham Gold Cup: L'Escargot (Tommy Carberry)

Motor Cycling

World 250 cc Champion: Rodney Gould

Motor Racing

Formula I Constructors Cup: Lotus

Rowing

Boat Race: Cambridge beat Oxford by 3¼ lengths

Rugby League

World Cup League Final: Australia 12, Great Britain 7

The Championship winners were St. Helens

The Challenge Cup winners were Castleford

Rugby Union

Tours Matches

South Africa 3, Scotland 6; South Africa 8, England 11; South Africa 8, Ireland 8; South Africa 6, Wales 6

International Championship

Champions: France and Wales shared
France 11, Scotland 9; France 8, Ireland 0; Wales 18, Scotland 9; England 9, Ireland 3; England 13, Wales 17; Ireland 16, Scotland 11; Ireland 14, Wales 0; Scotland 14, England 5; Wales 11, France 6; France 35, England 13

The County Champions were Staffordshire

Yachting

R.O.R.C. Points Championship

Class I   Noryema VII (R. W. Amey)
Class II   Blue Jacket III (D. J. Maw)
Class IV   Slipstream of Cowley (R.A.F. Association)

SAMURAI IN OVERALLS

Samurai: The Warrior caste of feudal Japan. Originated in the 9th century, when the Imperial Governments power to maintain order waned. Provincial classes were obliged to defend themselves under powerful chiefs to whom they held great loyalty. From the end of the 11th century until the middle of the 19th century government was exclusively in the hands of the samurai class.

The secret of the Japanese economic miracle

The author of our Japanese supplement: Dr. Peter Schmid (54), studied German language and literature, and history at Zurich University; after three years' school teaching and two years as dramatic adviser at the Berne Stadtheater, he became local editor of the Zurich daily "Tat" in 1944. In 1946 he became a features editor on the staff of the Swiss weekly "Weltwoche". One year later he started his career as globetrotter and political reporter which, during the following two decades, took him to almost every country in the world. He took up photography in 1955 and filming in 1960. As Far Eastern correspondent of a German TV programme he spent nearly four years in Tokyo. His books, which have been translated into a number of other languages, are characterized by an American critic as "giving the reader the maximum of information, yet making him feel, to a minimal degree, that he is being informed". His books "Japan Today" ("Japan heute"), "Spanish Impressions" ("Spanische Impressionen"), "Neighbours in the Sky" ("Nachbarn des Himmels", about South America), and "Paradise in the Jaws of the Dragon" ("Paradies im Drachenschlund", about South-East Asia) were published by the Deutsche Verlagsanstalt, "The Celestial Empire" ("Reich der Mitte", about Red China) by S. Fischer, and "India with and without Miracles" ("Indien mit und ohne Wunder") by Cotta. Peter Schmid has been Foreign Editor of the "Weltwoche" since spring 1969.

"Let us combine strength and spirit to build a new Japan. Let our hands do their utmost so what they achieve may be sent all over the world.
Harmony and sincerity!
Matsushita Electric!"

Every morning the phalanx of young workers of both sexes stand in front of their production line and sing this company song. Earlier they have performed physical exercises to improve their bodies, and this declaration of faith in their duty now provides the appropriate frame of mind as well. Practically all of them look alike, an impression which does not only arise from our tendency, as Westerners, to ignore the individual differences between the Oriental features, which are strange to us and which therefore appear rather uniform, but also from the atmosphere of collectivity which embraces the whole crowd. This atmosphere is enhanced by the identical light blue uniforms in which all of them are clad, including the engineer who conducted the choral creed from a rostrum, and even the factory manager. Individuals merge, more so than in the armed forces, where at least the officers stand out with their gold braid. The feeling, which one experiences in this largest and most modern factory in the world, producing television sets, is one of being in a human ant-heap in which the only thing of consequence is each individual's sober function. Compassionate references to the "ants" of Red China ignore the fact that capitalist Japan has a very similar human basis. The Confucian system, in which each person occupies a strictly defined position within a hierarchical system, governs human attitudes in both countries.

In the morning I was able to attend a meeting of the Board. Konsosuke Matsushita, the Chairman, calls his directors to this meeting every Monday morning. Here, too, the deferential atmosphere is most conspicuous, perpetuating the saintly authority of the ancient Chinese sage, and linked with the Japanese feudal tradition which makes it the samurai's inescapable duty to give his overlord unquestioning obedience. Matsushita, the largest tax-payer in Japan, is one of the most controversial figures among the crowd of businessmen who have created their industrial empires within the post-war economic miracle. He is one of the most modern among them yet, at the same time, one of those most adhering to tradition. He expresses his philosophy in a favourite anecdote of his. He once observed a tramp who was slaking his thirst at a well. This sight gave him a sudden revolutionary idea. Just as water, thanks to its abundance, is available to all who want it without any restriction whatsoever, mass production must lead to a situation when modern society is able to satisfy its everyday needs more and more cheaply, and in the end free of charge. Each according to his capabilities, to each according to his needs, as Marxist terminology expresses it. It is true that Matsushita, whose production lines disgorge electrical goods ranging from simple light switches to the rice cooker with automatic cut-off and colour television sets, has become a multi-millionaire during the achievement of this paradise-like state of affairs. But, precisely as the medieval *daimyo* acknowledged his patriarchal obligation towards his samurai, ready to sacrifice himself for his master, Japanese industrialists do not accept responsibility only for their balance-sheets, but also towards their workers, their country, and the world at large.

The doctrine of social harmony

In contrast to European industrial magnates who, as their responsibilities grow, have less and less time for relaxation and reflection and, at the height of their career, risk exhaustion and coronary attacks, Matsushita does not devote much time to the technical problems of his industrial empire. The latter he leaves to his directors who report, suggest and will accept the decisions of the boss without contradiction. On Monday

In Japan, the spirit behind the modern machines has remained wholly feudal. The same ceremony takes place in the Matsushita television factory every morning. Before they start, the workers stand in front of the production line and swear an oath, promising to work loyally and assiduously. The morning's ceremony ends with a hymn which, likewise, extols loyalty towards the firm.

afternoon I accompanied him to a quiet building in Japanese style, situated among temples, pine groves and ponds in the hilly surroundings of the ancient city of Kyoto, where he spends his days in the company of sociologists, psychologists and philosophers and ceremonially sips tea with them. "Capital and all that goes with a big enterprise are things which have only been borrowed from society and, therefore, they should not be treated as private property," was one of the fundamental findings of these discussions.

"It is the duty of every firm to make an adequate profit, but this profit must partly be restored to society and an endeavour needs to be made to satisfy the needs of the community." A few years ago Matsushita's PHP Research Institute (the letters stand for "Peace and Happiness through Prosperity"—the use of English is significant) was moved from the idyllic park in Kyoto to a modern building in the vicinity of the railway station, spreading the PHP philosophy henceforth by means of all the mass media. The world's most distinguished authors are invited to contribute to the PHP monthly which, with its millions of copies, proclaims the doctrine of social harmony. Soon it is to become available in translation to readers outside Japan. Ex oriente lux?

Like the boss, the workers, too, become philosophers. In the battery factory at Osaka, I was shown with pride the psychological advice centre for the staff, where a trained psychologist deals with the workers' personal problems just like in a modern European or American company. But the treatment administered is not to be found elsewhere. I entered a room the walls of which were covered with distorting mirrors. Arrows on the floor instructed the visitor in which direction he was to move, crosses where he was to pause. In one mirror one's reflection resembled a football, in the next a rake. The third showed a gigantic person on tiny legs, and so on. The profound comment of the psychologist interpreting this object lesson was "Mirrors deceive. Nobody

knows what he really looks like. Everything depends upon the position from which you look at it . . ." The following room has the effect of pushing the confused ego in the desired direction: stuffed dolls are placed along the walls and the worker is given a stick. "And now you hit them as hard as you can and think you are beating (the boss, the foreman? far from it)—yourself." Object: integration.

This lesson is successful. During my visit to Matsushita, which lasted several days, I had asked several times to meet representatives of the trade union. As is customary in Japan, I never received an outright refusal, but there was a kind of embarrassed silence every time. This attitude was all the more surprising, since Japanese trade unions do not cover a whole industry and do not, as powerful organizations in their own right, oppose the industrialists in negotiations concerning collective agreements. They are only company associations which cover the most disparate groups from the top echelons down to the unskilled workers. Even the parent organizations, among which the left-wing Socialist *Sohyo* is the strongest, are scarcely in a position to lead the fragmented groups, who lack homogeneity, into coherent action. Every year in the spring there is an offensive of strikes for higher wages, but its character is rather symbolic. The words "trade unions", in the patriarchal atmosphere of the early capitalism of the Japanese managers, sounds just as conspiratorial and subversive as the banding together of his samurai would have appeared suspicious to a war lord of the olden days. As was to be expected, the obstinacy of the management only made me all the more determined and, since I failed to make progress by using straightforward methods, I asked *Sohyo* for the private telephone number of the trade union representative at Matsushita Electric. "It is obvious that your boss does not want us to meet," I explained, anticipating the defiant and aggressive reaction which my disclosure would have triggered off in any Western trade union leader. But I was dis-

Despite their receptiveness for things new, the Japanese have profound respect for their cultural heritage. Ikebana (flower arrangement) has been developed into what is, in fact, an art which is still being learned by millions of Japanese women. Landscape gardening has reached a particularly high standard: the picture below shows the famous Seirenin garden in Kyoto. The women are playing the "koto", a typically Japanese musical instrument.

A little girl scatters lucky beans in front of a temple to celebrate the lunar New Year. In the background Tokyo's television tower.

The Japanese theatre is based upon a great tradition. In the Kabuki theatre, which had its beginnings in the early sixteenth century, men also perform the roles of women. In contrast to the No theatre, the actors wear heavy make-up instead of masks.

Extreme left-wing students, the so-called Zengakuren, are at the outer limits of the Japanese political spectrum. They frequently paralyse the functioning of the universities for months at a time.

appointed. "If Mr. Matsushita does not want us to meet," he said, "it would, in fact, be preferable that we should not meet . . ."

The power behind the throne

Even in the Japan of today, the word "to serve" still has almost magical significance. Just as the trade union leader, through the unwritten laws of loyalty, is linked with his boss, the latter, through a network of obligations, is linked with his staff and, beyond them, with the community and the nation at large. They serve it and its greatness, but they dominate it at the same time. Politics and industry are closely intertwined. When Japan, after her defeat, and without being involved in problems of defence, devoted all her energies and resources to peaceful economic expansion, and the campaigns for national regeneration were recorded on the economic charts instead of maps used by the general staff, *Keidanren*, which is the name of the Confederation of Japanese Industry, became something like the power behind the throne. "What is good for General Motors, is good for the country." This saying, which was widely ridiculed and questioned in the United States, would be accepted at its face value in Japan as a matter of course. What is to the liking of the "zaibatsus", the name given pre-war to the big industrial empires, disentangled by the victors in the name of democracy but reconstituted today in modified form, in the name of concentration, becomes the rule for the whole country. The leaders of the economy openly advocate the principle of "Non-separation of politics and economics", and the close integration of the state and the economy. The fact that the Liberal Democratic Party, which forms the Government, is financed by industry is considered self-evident rather than corrupt, as is the practice of ministers and senior civil servants to take up responsible positions in industry at the end of their careers. Captains of industry, senior public servants, and politicians, they are, after all,

products of the same few universities admission to which, in a way, represents the ticket to enter the realm of the élite. MITI (the Ministry of International Trade and Industry), in Japanese *Tsysynsho*, closely co-operates with the Confederation of Industry, within an economic system which almost ideally combines the advantages of market economy-orientated free enterprise and the purposefulness of a centrally directed planned economy. On the basis of long-term economic plans and estimates of requirements, MITI issues guidelines which are intended to minimize unsound investments and make the best use of available resources. MITI does not refrain from protecting domestic industries by import restrictions and Customs tariffs, brazenly diluting the liberalization demanded by the whole world into mere lip-service, and setting rigorous limits for foreign investment. (Not more than 20 per cent of the capital of a Japanese firm is made available to foreign capitalists.) There is no doubt that, measured by capacity and rates of growth, Japan has the smallest share of foreign investment among the highly developed industrial nations (it should be noted that, immediately after the United States, Switzerland is in the second position). However, within the guidelines set by MITI and reinforced by official credit policy, private firms are permitted to engage in a type of competition which knows no pity, recalling the blood feuds of the Middle Ages. Government direction and intensive private competition have created the Japanese economic miracle of today. "The most intelligent dirigiste system in the world today," according to the *Economist* in an admiring and rather envious statement.

The richest country in the world in 2005?

"It would be far from surprising if the 21st century would be that of Japan," runs the prophecy of the American futurologist Herman Kahn of the Hudson Institute; and in its issue

294

The tea ceremony is one of Japan's great traditions, developed from the meditation exercises of the Zen doctrine.

Worshippers in front of the Yasukini Temple in Tokyo, which is dedicated to those killed in wars (far right).

dated 19th March 1969, the highly respected Japanese financial journal *Nihon Keizai*, on the basis of a forecast by the Ministry of Finance, announced with banner headlines: "Japan will be the richest country in the world". But only in 2005, and provided that the current growth rates (between 12 and 14 per cent annually) continue. These rates have enabled the small and tenacious sprinter from the Far East to overtake, at a steady pace, all competitors during the last few years. The gross national product of Japan dislodged that of the Federal Republic of Germany from third place in the global stakes in 1968. In fifteen years' time at the latest, in 1984/85, it will be the turn of the Soviet Union to be overtaken. And in the U.S.A., unless a miracle boosts the relatively low average growth rate of 4·7 per cent (during the past eight years), Herman Kahn's vision will have become reality by the turn of the century and Japan will be the *Sekai dai-ichi*, the first nation in the world.

This will be based on her *per capita* income as well as her ranking as a nation, even though the distance from the top is much further, since Japan's *per capita* income ranks twentieth! In other words, wealth is not, as yet, fairly distributed and there are, as yet, too many people claiming their share of the cake for individuals to achieve prosperity. The Mr. Suzuki of today has to make do with a little house made of wood, glass and paper into which he has to squeeze with his family: the *tatami* (the name of the straw mats covering the floor) cover only a few square metres. And for his meals, he has to be satisfied with a bowl of rice or noodles and a tiny piece of fish. In 2001, however, he will be the richest man in the world, twice as rich as the Swede, the runner-up (who will have overtaken today's leader, the American, as early as 1976), four times as rich as the American, and six times as rich as the Swiss. It all seems difficult to imagine.

And that is the future before a nation which suffered total defeat in 1945, had 80 per cent of her productive capacity destroyed, saw her territory reduced by almost half, had to contend with the return of millions of soldiers and expatriate Japanese, was endowed with a social structure which had been shaken to its foundations, and was unable to see even a glimmer of hope on the horizon. The German economic miracle pales into insignificance in the face of this Japanese super-achievement. Even fifty years ago, Europeans could afford to look upon the Japanese "dumping" on world markets with contempt: "made in Japan" simply stood for cheap, second-rate goods that were shamelessly copied by people devoid of creative initiative of their own. This prejudice is so deeply rooted that the myth of Japanese "starvation wages" is still widely accepted as explanation for the unexpected ability to compete. Such assessments have to be thoroughly revised.

Imitation honours the example

The days when Canon copied Leica and Nikon copied Contax so closely that the spare parts of German and Japanese cameras became interchangeable, are no longer with us. The German designers, who were resting on their laurels, have since been displaced from world markets by their Japanese competitors who had more readily grasped that, in these hectic times, it was essential to let the models get out of date, by introducing a steady stream of new ideas and alterations, and to strive after mass production instead of producing cameras that last for a lifetime. When, in this context, imitation simplifies the process of development, the Japanese are nowadays as ruthless as ever. Those, however, who are familiar with Oriental ways of thinking, are reluctant to pronounce the moral judgement inherent in the term "ruthless". The need to memorize thousands of Chinese ideographs in early childhood has forced the Japanese to adopt an attitude which assigns to memory a more important function than logical thinking, and which considers the closest possible

This girl emerged from a painting contest as a remarkable child artist. Her motif is one of the most beautiful temples in her home town of Kyoto.

Cherry blossom time, which transforms parks and gardens, is the occasion of a popular festival.

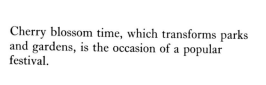

Rice is still the staple diet of the Japanese.
The annual harvest is able to supply 90 per cent
of the demand, the rest has to be imported.
The picture on the right-hand page shows the
hard toil in a paddy field on the Chiba
peninsula.

The Tokaido line, most
modern rail route in the
world, pride and symbol
of the world's third-
largest industrial power.
The super-express, which
takes 190 minutes to
cover 515 km, heralded
the comeback of the
railways.

Commuter traffic in
Tokyo: each journey to
work turns into a
merciless fight for space.
Passengers being literally
pressed into the carriages.

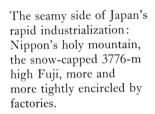

The seamy side of Japan's rapid industrialization: Nippon's holy mountain, the snow-capped 3776-m high Fuji, more and more tightly encircled by factories.

imitation as the paramount virtue in the process of learning. In the life of any European working with Japanese assistants there are moments when, in despair, he has to doubt their intelligence. Take the occasion when they may be asked to summarize a book or a newspaper article into a few pages or sentences. In the opinion of many Western educationists, with whom I have discussed the hair-raising results of such tasks, the Japanese find it easier to learn whole pages by heart than to recognize and condense the essential theme. To a Japanese, then, imitation honours rather than impairs the example. And if it is at all possible to improve a detail of the borrowed principle (a phase which was often reached before a more original attitude was adopted), this step is even considered meritorious.

The piratical indifference towards foreign patents has quite naturally been replaced by a more correct attitude since Japan began to expose the Western arrogance, which considered the Japanese incapable of ever displaying creative originality, by producing genuine innovations. What I have in mind above all is the revolutionary shipbuilding technique of laying down the keel in separate parts and joining them together afterwards. The fact that the Japanese, with regard to completion dates and prices, have been able to undercut the shipyards of the whole world is exclusively based on the inventiveness of Japanese engineers.

The "technological gap" closes

It cannot be denied, however—and the Japanese are the last to harbour illusions about this—that, as far as technology is concerned, they are, as yet, forced to a large extent to rely on Western licences. But this dependence is beginning to weaken or may even be reversed. I can illustrate this by giving three examples of epoch-making achievements which were highlighted in the press in the summer of 1969 underlining, so to speak, the significance of the centenary of the Meiji

revolution which heralded the modern development of Japan. Directly or indirectly, all three examples are related to steel, which symbolizes modern progress. In July of 1969 the atomic energy commission of the Japanese Iron and Steel Association announced the first results of research which made the manufacture of steel by using nuclear energy a definite possibility. This means that Japan, hitherto obliged to import hundreds of millions of tons of expensive coke essential for the manufacture of steel, would achieve much lower production costs and become a considerably stronger competitor in world markets.

It was in the same July of 1969 that the German firm of Klöcknerwerke AG announced that they had purchased the modern hot rolled broad strip method, developed by the Japanese steel firm Yawata, for their works at Bremen. At the same time, during the meeting of the Japanese Metallurgical Association at the city of Sendai, the research team of the Ishikawashima Heavy Industries (the shipyards of which, incidentally, were also pioneers in the construction of giant tankers) announced that they had produced steel with a tensile strength that was greatly superior to that of the special steel used for U.S. jet aircraft. Significantly, the technique employed was similar to that used in the smoky workshops of the sword-makers on Shikoku island for centuries: thin layers of iron made of different alloys are placed on top of each other and welded together. Not only intellectually, but also technologically, the distance between contemporary Japan and her traditional roots is a short one.

The period when foreign designs were copied or there was reliance upon licensing agreements has been followed by a leap into self-reliance. After the first American computer had been imported in 1957, the Japanese marketed their first machines two years later, still based on foreign know-how. The Nippon Electric Co. was associated with Honeywell, Hitachi with RCA, Toshiba and Mitsubishi with General Electric, and Oki with

When it comes to left-wing tendencies, it is mainly the Zengakuren student movement which represents Japan's extra-parliamentary opposition. During recent years, however, it has lost much of its former impact.

Bottom: Sapporo, capital of Hokkaido island, during the snow festival. The Olympic Winter Games will be staged here in 1972.

There are more than 300 officially recognized religious denominations in Japan. Shinto is Japan's most ancient religion and still enjoys the largest support. Buddhism is the second most important. Many Japanese, however, are Shintoists and Buddhists at the same time. The most beautiful and colourful religious feasts are those of the Shintoists: below the shrine procession of the "Big Drum" in Osaka, left the feast of the Meiji shrine in Tokyo, centre left temple virgins at the imperial shrine of the sun-goddess Amaterasu at Ise.

Above: the Ama divers from the fishing village of Onjuku, on the east coast of the Chiba peninsula, on their way to work. They dive for shells and seaweed.

Geishas entertaining customers in a tea-house with music, singing and dancing. The geisha's position in Japanese social life has often been misunderstood in the West.

A Zen Buddhist priest at the Daisen Temple of Kyoto. This temple is famous for its rock garden, designed in 1509 by Kogaku Soko in strict accordance with the philosophy of Zen Buddhism. The thoughts of the priest, whose everyday existence corresponds fairly closely to that of the temple's founder, are none the less directed towards modern Japan.

Univac. Today, ten years later, these Japanese firms have made themselves to a large extent independent. The computers dealing with accounts and inventories, reserving seats for transport enterprises, and co-ordinating time-tables in the Japan of today are largely of Japanese manufacture. In the absence of defence contracts there are no large computers, as there are in the United States where development costs are based on such contracts, but when it comes to mini-computers, the Japanese are in the lead. Their new models do not require air-conditioning and are operated by ordinary electric current, which makes them extremely versatile: they can cope with scientific/technological calculations as well as chemical analyses in hospital laboratories.

In space travel, too, Japan now occupies third place after the United States and the Soviet Union, Europe having got nowhere because of her lack of direction. It is true that the three-stage Mu-3D only went into orbit from its launching pad at the southern end of Kyushu island ·after the first two launches had failed, but the eventual success not only entitles Japan to hope that she will be able to do without the expensive U.S. communications and research satellites, but also that, in the not too distant future, she will have her own nuclear rockets and thus will be able to compete with China, a nuclear power.

It must be conceded that Japan still imports ten times as many licences as she exports but, during the last five years, the export of patents rose ten times as fast as their import. In other words, the use of Japanese patents abroad rose by 500 per cent within five years while the use of foreign patents in Japan increased by only 50 per cent during the same period. The "technological gap" is likely to close even more rapidly in the near future, after completion of the new "city of learning and science", which is in the process of construction not far from Tokyo, and will house 160,000 engineers, research workers and philosophers.

Creative destruction

Japan's Government and the managers of her private sector are not only prepared to invest immense sums in research but also to use investments, to a much larger extent than the more careful and more conservative Europeans, to keep their productive capacity up to scratch. The term they have coined for this attitude is self-explanatory: "creative destruction". Before the existing plant has been fully written off, there is a rush for new loans (which, again and again, are readily granted by enterprising bankers). Always the newest, the most modern: that is the mania which is also prevalent in the developing countries, where it is the result of an obvious inferiority complex. Maybe this complex also affects the Japanese, without their being prepared to admit it, just like the lack of assurance of the social climber, except that he has become more rather than less confident. "Since we are, technologically speaking, without a past," declared the celebrated motor-cycle manufacturer Shoichiro Honda, "we must make do with the future. Basically, we were lucky that we lost the war, otherwise we would never have gained the freedom we are enjoying today. We were able to start from scratch and choose wide perspectives."

As to the "low wages" of their workers, about which so much has been written, Japanese industrialists call it a trumped-up problem: if everything that the large firms do for the welfare of their workers, behind the scenes, is taken into account, their position lies somewhere between that of their French and Italian fellow-workers.

This statement, however, is not the whole truth, since the statistics only cover the regular workforce of the modern factories, ignoring the auxiliaries and casual workers who do not belong to "the family" and the much more numerous workers in the small firms which still make up two-thirds of the Japanese workers.

The "Atom Dome" of Hiroshima reminds the Japanese of the darkest hour in their recent history. It is one of the most interesting phenomena of our time that it is Japan and Germany, the two all-out losers of 1945, which have attracted widespread envy by achieving economic miracles.

The Shinto shrine of Izumo in winter. Many young couples are married in this temple.

The feast of the Sanja shrine is one of the most attractive and interesting in Japan's capital. The bearers of the heavy and precious shrines achieve a state of ecstasy during the procession.

Participants in the feast of purification of Hakodate, which is held at the depth of winter in snow and freezing temperature, have to be in tough physical condition.

Returning from a temple festival on Kurama mountain near Kyoto with a lucky bamboo cane.

Rewards for loyalty to the firm

Wages for the "élite workers" of large firms like Matsushita, Canon, or Honda rose by an average of 10 per cent during the last decade, far more than the rise in prices. Between 1957 and 1967, the salary of a newly graduated engineer more than doubled, that of a new entrant with secondary education trebled. Once a person steps over the threshold of a large enterprise, he generally stays there for the rest of his life, like a samurai who becomes a part of the entourage of his overlord. His wages constantly rise, year after year, as long as he remains with the firm, even when the length of service begins to have an adverse effect on his performance. What he is paid for is not really his performance, but the fact that he belongs to the large company family.

If the firm is doing well, the worker benefits from the bonus, representing a share in the profits, which is paid twice yearly, at New Year and in the summer. This bonus can be as much as a month's salary each year in the case of rich firms. This is without mentioning numerous other benefits which cannot be quantified easily: homes at ridiculously low rents, allowances for transport and clothing, free medical treatment, company holiday homes and recreational organizations which give instruction in all kinds of things, from the ceremonies linked with serving tea for young girls to single-stick combat for young men. And when these young people pair off and get married, the firm not infrequently stages a collective wedding.

Thus far the advantages of belonging to the family. But when it comes to changing jobs in Japan, even if it means bettering oneself, this is regarded as causing the same embarrassment as a divorce in our bourgeois society. A recent survey indicates that, for men over 20 years of age, changing jobs in urban areas accounts for only 1·04 per cent! The reasons for this are not merely sentimental but also realistic: at the absurdly low

age of retirement of 55 years, the lump sum paid out—there is no pension—equals the number of monthly salaries corresponding to the number of years served with the firm. Furthermore, only very few people retire in the strict sense of the word. Those who have given loyal service are rewarded by finding refuge with one of the subsidiary companies of the firm (which are frequently operated for this very purpose, like a siding).

It stands to reason that this loyalty to the firm, as well as the salary scale based on seniority rather than performance, counteract psychological incentive and the efficiency of a modern enterprise. The more modern industrialists are beginning to strive for a reform of these archaic methods of management, but it is safe to assume that they will never be completely abandoned.

In the factory run by Mr. Nagano in Asakusa, which produces rubber sheeting for cars, one gets the impression of having been taken back a hundred years. Indeed, one wonders whether it is right to refer to a "factory", since one experiences a lot of trouble in locating the address among a maze of small streets blocked with boxes and vehicles. Beneath a picturesque sign in Chinese lettering there is a sliding door giving direct access to the firm—right in the private house of Mr. Nagano. The *tatami* in the front rooms have been removed and replaced by the work-benches where some two dozen young people are at work under a few neon lights suspended from the ceiling. Mrs. Nagano is making tea in the background. The furthering of the family spirit practised by big firms applies even more strongly in this case: most of the employees are cousins who have moved to Tokyo from the country to help their uncle. To obtain wage statistics is a hopeless venture here, since factory inspectors rarely if ever turn up, even if the working hours, as easily happens in such a family atmosphere, stretch late into the night. If business is bad, the

Karate (right) originated in the island of Okinawa. Like judo it is a sport teaching the art of self-defence and has gained a growing number of adherents in the West. The sumo fighters are typically Japanese and enjoy an unrivalled popularity. The picture shows some of the rising sumo generation, as yet well proportioned, during their daily fitness training.

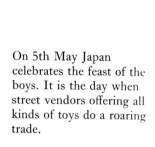

On 5th May Japan celebrates the feast of the boys. It is the day when street vendors offering all kinds of toys do a roaring trade.

employees are grateful to have at least a roof over their heads and to receive their daily bowl of rice and noodles. What we have here, right in the centre of modern Tokyo, is an ancient Asian type of artisanal enterprise, with antediluvian machines which, worked by hand, cut various shapes out of sheets of rubber. Difficult though it is to believe, the big car manufacturers of Toyota and Nissan are supplied from here. These hypermodern factories, like similar ones in other industries, are nothing but the visible and shining tip of an iceberg, the invisible body of which consists of innumerable small supply units. When exports are thriving, the Naganos enjoy a measure of prosperity; when there is a decline in sales, the small suppliers are the first to feel the effects of the crisis. Unless, that is, they are not already affected by the tightening of the screw, since the growing shortage of labour, which also manifests itself in Japan, encourages the young generation in disregard of family solidarity, to seek work at the big factories. The small firms are only able to carry on by linking with each other and modernizing. Thus the iceberg slowly rises from the sea; the Asian base of the small industries begins to assume Western appearance. Some products requiring a large amount of manual work, which used to constitute a considerable proportion of the exports to the United States and Europe, are no longer economic today, being undersold by competitors elsewhere in Asia, such as Korea and Hong Kong . . .

Cheap labour? Its advantages are mostly offset by primitive conditions of production, although there is one case when this does not apply: that of the countless girls and young women who, from Sony's production lines to Canon's assembly desks, solder transistor radios and screw camera casings together with their quick and elastic hands, who are always cheerfully smiling, bringing the perennial grace of the butterfly to the factory. Without enjoying the long-standing privileges of their male fellow-workers, they

cheaply perform first-class work. And when they have saved enough for their trousseau, they abandon industry for the role of housewife and mother.

Catastrophic neglect of the problems of the environment

What of the future of the island kingdom? Will the Japanese miracle continue relentlessly, at an undiminished pace? Will Tokyo become the capital of the world? There are limitations which may put the brake on "Icarus flying towards the sun" and curb the fantastic dreams.

Japan has paid for her phenomenal rise with an almost criminal neglect of her substructures. What would be the use of reaching the highest standard of living in the world while sustaining biological damage in the process? The contamination of the environment, which is threatening to choke all industrial nations, is more ruthless in Japan than in any other country. Even today she produces nine times as much as the United States per square kilometre, owns almost three times as many motor vehicles for the same area and shed twelve times as much blood in road accidents in 1969. One inhabitant in five in the capital is suffering from one of more than forty symptoms of chronic bronchitis resulting from aerial pollution. Public investment has been hopelessly out-distanced in the chase after super-production in the private sector. (For instance, while the number of cars rose five times during ten years, the road system increased by a mere 6 per cent.) The catastrophic conditions of the environment have now become so alarming that the Government has proclaimed suitable action one of the most pressing tasks. No country can transgress its biological frontiers forever: despite everything, there is a limit even for Japan's road ahead.

The photographs in this supplement were taken by Peter Schmid, Erhard Hürsch, Hans W. Silvester, Henry Hymans, Georg Gerster and Per-Olle Stackman.

The most imposing
building in the ancient
imperial city of Nara,
Japan's capital from
710 to 784, is the
Daibutsuden Hall of the
Todaiji Temple, which
houses a Buddha statue
almost 16 m high.
Hundreds of stags,
protected since time
immemorial, populate the
temple precincts.

Biographies

Allende, Salvador, born 26th July, 1908, in Santiago, in Chile, studied medicine and became a student leader in the fight against the régime of President Ibañez. A year before qualifying as a doctor he was elected a deputy for the province of Valparaiso, but was also active in various official organizations concerned with health and was co-author of a number of publications on health matters and the national health service. In 1939 he became Minister of Health in a Popular Front government and remained in this post until 1942. In 1943 he became Vice-Chairman and Manager of the Workers' Health Insurance Fund. In the same year he became General Secretary of the "Partido Socialista", which he had helped to found, and was elected to the Senate. In 1952 he ran as a Presidential candidate for the first time, after having founded a "Frente del Pueblo" (Popular Front) which, apart from his own Socialist Party, included a number of small left-wing parties. The mere 57,000 votes he obtained failed to discourage him, for he tried again in 1958. This time, although women who owed their votes to him were able to participate in a Presidential election for the first time, thereby enabling him to gain 356,000 votes, he was still narrowly defeated by a Conservative, Jorge Alessandri. Allende extended his "Popular Front" by forming a coalition with the Communists, but was beaten by the Christian Democrat Eduardo Frei in the 1964 Presidential election. It was only at the fourth try that he achieved his objective, gaining the largest number of votes (1,075,616 or 36·3 per cent) in the Presidential election of 4th September, 1970. Since none of the candidates had obtained an absolute majority Congress had to elect the President, in accordance with the constitution. When his successful opponent of 1958, whom Allende had now narrowly beaten into second place,

withdrew his candidature, Congress ceremonially endorsed Allende as President on 24th October, 1970. On 3rd November he assumed his functions. Allende, despite his left-wing political views and support of Castro, is a millionaire with a stake in a number of different businesses. He wants to follow a "Chilean path" to socialism.

Gierek, Edward, born 6th January, 1913, in the village of Porabka. His father was a miner, killed in a mine accident while Edward was still a child. In 1923 his mother emigrated to France where the young Edward started work in a coal-mine at the early age of 13. He soon became an active trade unionist and joined the French Communist Party in 1931. He was the principal organizer of the first sit-down strike in French history and was deported to Poland in 1934, where he was then called up for military service. In 1939 Gierek emigrated to Belgium and once more became a miner and Communist agitator. During the German occupation of Belgium he was active in the underground movement. After the war he became Chairman of the National Council of Poles in Belgium. In 1948 he returned to his native Poland and took up a Communist Party post in the Katowice Voivodship. His rapid rise within the Party apparatus started in the fifties. At the same time he studied at the Cracow Academy of Mining, obtaining his diploma in engineering in 1954. In the same year he became a parliamentary deputy and a member of the Central Committee of the Polish United Workers' Party. From 1955 to 1956 he was in charge of the section for heavy industry at the Secretariat of the Central Committee in Warsaw. In 1956 he also belonged to the Politburo for some months but did not finally join it on a definite basis until 1959. In addition, he had become Party Secretary in Katowice in 1957. The Party leadership in highly industrialized Upper Silesia, the pivot of Poland's economy, placed him in a key position. Gierek, renowned as an able administrator and economist, used it as a power base from which to pursue a cautious policy of reform. The revolt

by the workers in the Baltic ports in December 1970, which swept the old guard in Warsaw out of office, offered Gierek his great opportunity: as Wladyslaw Gomulka's successor, he became Poland's new Party Leader on 20th December.

Heath, Edward Richard George, born 9th July, 1916, in Broadstairs, the son of a carpenter. He studied philosophy, politics and economics at Oxford, where he was Chairman of the Conservative Club, and President of the Union in 1939. After the outbreak of war Heath volunteered for the Army and, as a gunner in the Royal Artillery, saw service in France, Belgium, the Netherlands and Germany, attaining the rank of Lieutenant-Colonel and gaining a number of decorations. After leaving the Forces he first worked for the Ministry of Civil Aviation and then joined a merchant bank. He subsequently devoted himself mainly to politics. In the general election of 1950 he was elected, by a narrow majority, to represent the London suburb of Bexley. From 1955 onwards he occupied the posts of Conservative Chief Whip and Parliamentary Secretary to the Treasury. In October 1959, he became a member of the government for the first time, and became Minister of Labour. Nine months later he was appointed Lord Privy Seal, with Foreign Office responsibilities. When Great Britain applied to join the Common Market in 1961, Heath was placed in charge of the British negotiating team. Although the negotiations failed in January 1963, as a result of de Gaulle's veto, Heath's efforts won much acclaim; the German city of Aachen awarded him the Charlemagne Prize. In October 1963, Heath became Secretary of State for Industry, Trade and Regional Development in the Douglas-Home government. After the 1964 Labour victory, he became Conservative Party Leader and Leader of the Opposition in the House of Commons in 1965. He lost the election in 1966 but, confounding all prophets, emerged as the victor in the election of 1970. Appointed Prime Minister by the Queen, Edward Heath became the first bachelor Prime Minister for over sixty years to take possession of No. 10 Downing Street.

Kreisky, Bruno, born 22nd January, 1911, in Vienna, the son of an industrialist. As a schoolboy of 15 he joined the Socialist Youth Movement and, while studying law, became Chairman of the Central Committee of the "Revolutionäre Sozialistische Jugend". He joined the Sozialistische Partei Österreichs (SPÖ) and occupied a leading position when it went underground after having been banned in 1934 following serious disorders. He was arrested for illegal political activity in 1935, and was tried and found guilty of high treason in 1936. Although he spent several months in prison, he was able to graduate in law in 1937. After Austria was overrun by Germany, Kreisky was arrested by the Gestapo in 1938 and sentenced to five months in prison. After his release he succeeded in escaping to Sweden where he worked as an economist in the co-operative movement, and as a journalist. After the end of the war Kreisky returned to Austria, entered the Austrian Foreign Service in 1946 and joined the staff of the Austrian Embassy in Stockholm. After two years in the economic department of the Foreign Ministry, he became an aide to President Körner in 1951. In April 1953, Kreisky became State Secretary, dealing with foreign affairs, in the Prime Minister's office and, in that capacity, took a leading part in the negotiations culminating in Austria's recovery of her independence. In July 1959, he was appointed Foreign Minister in the third Raab cabinet and grappled with the problem of South Tyrol. After his party had been beaten in the general election of March 1966, resulting in the dissolution of the Grand Coalition, Kreisky ceased to be a member of the government but was elected Party Leader in February 1967, in succession to Pittermann. In the general election of 1st March, 1970, the SPÖ obtained the largest number of seats and Kreisky, as architect of the victory, was entrusted by President Jonas with the task of forming a coalition government. When, however, the negotiations with the People's Party

failed, Prime Minister Kreisky formed an SPÖ minority government on 19th April. Kreisky, whose wife is Swedish, is considered a supporter of "active neutrality".

Meir, Golda, born as the daughter of a fisherman named Mabovitch, on 3rd May, 1898, in Kiev, in the Ukraine. She grew familiar with pogroms in her childhood. At the age of six she took part in the funeral rites for 45 murdered Jews. In 1906 her parents emigrated to the United States where her father found work in Milwaukee as a carpenter. It was there that Golda Meir went to school and later attended the Teachers' Seminary. She subsequently worked as a teacher and librarian in Milwaukee, Chicago and New York. When she married the Zionist Morris Myerson in Denver, she made the condition that they should move to Palestine, which was then under British administration. From 1921 onwards they made their living by running a chicken farm at the kibbutz of Merhavia, and she studied Hebrew and Arabic. In 1926 she was elected a member of the Women's Labour Council, and later of the executive committee, of the Histraduth, the trade union organization, which she represented at several international conferences. She rapidly made a name for herself as an energetic politician. Elected to the executive committee of the Jewish Agency as a representative of Mapai, Golda Meir became the Head of the Agency's Political Department in 1946. In 1948, in an attempt to prevent the outbreak of war between the Israelis and Arabs she travelled through hostile territory, disguised as an Arab woman, and negotiated with King Abdullah of Transjordan. Although her efforts were unsuccessful, since the King gave way to pressure from the other Arab leaders, Golda Meir's courage impressed the Arabs. On 14th May, 1948, she was one of the signatories of the proclamation of the new state of Israel. She was the only woman in the first provisional government and, in June of the same year, was sent to represent her country in Moscow as Israel's first Ambassador. In March 1949, she became Minister of Labour and Social

Insurance, created progressive social and old-age insurance, and solved the tremendous problem of finding work for almost a million immigrants. In June 1956, she became Moshe Sharett's successor as Minister of Foreign Affairs and retained the post in several governments headed by Ben Gurion and Levi Eshkol. For many years she was close to Ben Gurion, who once called her "the only man in the cabinet". At the end of December 1965, for health reasons, she ceded her post as Minister of Foreign Affairs to Abba Eban, but a few months later she was elected Secretary-General of Mapai. She relinquished this post in February 1968, but remained a member of the Knesset, the Israeli parliament. After Prime Minister Eshkol suddenly died of a stroke on 26th February, 1969, Golda Meir, the grandmother, was asked to be Head of Government and was confirmed as Prime Minister by the Knesset on 17th March, 1969. Following Sirimavo Bandaranaike and Indira Gandhi, Golda Meir became the third woman to head a government.

Nasser, Gamal Abdel, born 15th January, 1918, in Upper Egypt, son of a postal official. Early in his life he joined a patriotic organization and was arrested because of "subversive activities" in Cairo when he was 17. Although he later participated in antimonarchist demonstrations and was badly injured in a clash with the police in the mid-thirties, he was authorized to attend the Military Academy in 1937 and became a Lieutenant in 1940. As a Major he particularly distinguished himself in the war against Israel in 1948, but was subsequently taken prisoner. He played a leading role in the "Committee of Free Officers" which, under the leadership of General Neguib, deposed King Farouk on 26th July, 1952, and was appointed Commander-in-Chief of the Armed Forces. When the monarchy was abolished in Egypt on 18th July, 1953, Nasser advanced to the position of Deputy Prime Minister and Minister of the Interior. When Neguib was dropped, in a surprise move, on 25th February, 1954, and Nasser was named his successor, there followed a brief struggle for power in which the armed forces supported Nasser. On 14th November, 1954, Nasser also dismissed Neguib as Head of State and assumed his functions himself. After Nasser had nationalized the Suez Canal on 26th July, 1956, the "punitive expedition" of Great Britain, France and Israel ended in failure, due to the opposition of the United States and the Soviet Union. Despite Nasser's growing prestige in the Arab world his favourite project, the union of all Arab states in the form of the "United Arab Republic", under his leadership, failed again and again. The U.A.R. Federal State, created in February 1958, after having been endorsed by referenda in Egypt and Syria, which was also joined by Yemen, disintegrated in 1961 after a military coup in Damascus. After the outbreak of civil war in Yemen in 1962, Nasser gave the Republicans massive support by sending troops and supplies without, however, gaining any benefit. Nasser made his hostility to Israel the vehicle of his pan-Arab aspirations. In May 1967, after he had forced the U.N. troops to withdraw, he provoked Israel, by closing the Straits of Tiran and massing troops in the Sinai peninsula, into a preventive strike which unleashed the Six-Day War between Israel and the Arab states. Within a few days Israel restored access to the Gulf of Aqaba, occupied East Jerusalem and Western Jordan, wrested the Golan Heights from the Syrians and drove the Egyptians, who suffered heavy losses, back across the Suez Canal. After this humiliating defeat Nasser wanted to resign on 9th June, 1967, but changed his mind the following day. Ten days later he added the posts of Head of Government and Secretary-General of the Arab Socialist Union, the official party created by himself, to that of President. Nasser's endeavours to neutralize the effects of the defeat of 1967 made him constantly more dependent upon the Soviet Union, which not only constructed the Aswan Dam for him but also assumed a leading role in military matters. Two events which made the redoubtable "troublemaker" of the fifties and sixties appear as a statesman in search of peace occurred at the end

of his life: despite strong resistance among Arabs, he agreed to the Rogers peace plan and, 24 hours before his sudden death, he succeeded in his role of mediator in the Jordanian civil war. Nasser died of a coronary thrombosis on 28th September, 1970.

Sadat, Anwar, born 25th December, 1918, in Meit-Abu el-Kom on the Nile delta, chose a military career. At the provincial garrison of Mankabad, before the Second World War, he met Nasser, a fellow officer. Together they founded the conspiratorial group of the "Free Officers" which was to overthrow the monarchy in 1952. In 1942 during the war, Sadat was arrested and expelled from the Egyptian Army because of his pro-Nazi sympathies. In 1945 the British arrested him once more, accusing him of having taken part in a plot against Prime Minister Nahas Pasha. In 1952 he was one of the leaders in the officers' conspiracy which planned the coup against King Farouk. Promoted Colonel, he played a leading part in the Revolutionary Council, founded the official newspaper "Al Goumhouria" and became Minister of Information in Nasser's second government in 1954. After losing this post in a government reshuffle, he was entrusted with the preparatory work for the creation of an official party. This was established in 1957 as the "National Union" with Sadat as Secretary-General. In 1960 he became President of the National Assembly. He was also active in the foundation of the "Arab Socialist Union" (ASU) which replaced the "National Union" in 1962. At the end of 1969 Sadat was appointed Vice-President of the U.A.R. After Nasser's sudden death on 28th September, 1970, he became Acting President. Nominated as Nasser's successor by the official party, he was elected President, unopposed, on 15th October, 1970.

Scheel, Walter, born 8th July, 1919, in Solingen, the son of a wheelwright. After training for a banking career, he was called up and spent the Second World War as a night fighter pilot, reaching the rank of Lieutenant. After the end of the war he went into

industry and from 1945 until 1953 he worked as a senior executive for a steel firm. He then set up on his own as a business consultant in Düsseldorf. Scheel joined the Free Democrats (FDP) in 1946, becoming a member of the Düsseldorf local council in 1948, and of the Landtag of North Rhine-Westphalia in 1950. In 1953 he was elected as a member of the Bundestag. In 1956 he was one of the "Young Turks" who played a leading part in the fall of the CDU/FDP Land government of North Rhine-Westphalia, which was replaced by a coalition with the Social Democrats. In October 1961 Scheel, who since 1958 had been the manager of a Düsseldorf finance house which he had helped to found, and who had become known as an expert in development aid problems, accepted the newly formed Federal Ministry for Economic Co-operation in the Adenauer government. He continued in this post in the first and second Erhard governments. After Erhard's fall, when all FDP Ministers left the government, Scheel became Vice-President of the Bundestag. In January 1968 he was elected Party Chairman of the Free Democrats in succession to Erich Mende. The FDP steered a distinctly reformist course under its new leader, advocating an active Ostpolitik, a treaty with the German Democratic Republic (which implied renunciation of the claim that the Federal Republic was the sole German state), and an all-European security conference. This markedly progressive line was not, however, endorsed by the electors in the 1969 general election, but the FDP rejoined the government as junior partner of the Social Democrats despite the serious set-back. Walter Scheel became Minister of Foreign Affairs and Vice-Chancellor in the Social/Liberal government which Willy Brandt, the new Chancellor, formed in October 1969. The signing of the Non-Proliferation Treaty and the new initiatives towards the East were evidence of the new outlook. In spite of the strong resistance offered by the CDU/CSU Opposition, Brandt and Scheel signed treaties with the Soviet Union and Poland in 1970.

INDEX of personalities

INDEX of events